# FISCAL FEDERALISM IN INDIA

# FISCAL FEDERALISM IN INDIA

**Dr. KUMARI REKHA**
Dr. Ram Manohar Lohiya Smarak Mahavidyalaya,
Muzaffarpur
(A Constituent Unit of B.R.A. Bihar University, Muzaffarpur)

**REGAL PUBLICATIONS**
New Delhi-110027

FISCAL FEDERALISM IN INDIA

ISBN 978-81-8484-302-6



*Typeset by*
S.S. COMPOSERS
3190, Mohindra Park, Shakur Basti, Delhi-110034.

*Printed in India at*
MAYUR ENTERPRISES
WZ Plot No. 3, Gujjar Market, Tihar Village, New Delhi-110018.

*Published by*
REGAL PUBLICATIONS
F-159, Rajouri Garden, New Delhi-110027.
Phone: +91-11-45546396
E-mail: regalbookspub@yahoo.com

# Contents

Preface ix

1. CONCEPT OF FISCAL FEDERALISM 1
   - (I) Political Base of Fiscal Federalism 1
     - History of Feseralism and the Federal Idea 3
     - Federal Principles 9
     - Characteristics of Federal Systems 11
   - (II) Nature of the Indian Federal System 17
   - (III) Economic Interpretation of Federalism 19
   - (IV) Bargaining Process under Federal Set-up 20
   - (V) Problem of Fiscal Adjustments 23
   - (VI) Guiding Principles of Fiscal Adjustments 24
   - (VII) Federal Inter-Regional Transference of Resources and Economic Development 25
   - (VIII) Federal Finance and Economic Development 27

2. UNION-STATE FISCAL RELATION IN INDIA 32
   - (I) Brief Survey of Union-State Fiscal Relation before Government of India Act, 1935 32
   - (II) Financial Provisions under Government of India Act, 1935 36
     - Borrowing and Audit 39
     - Audit and Accounts 39
     - Financial Power of the Governor 40
     - Income Tax 41
     - Review of Financial Relations 43
   - (III) Financial Power Under Indian Constitution 46
     - Borrowing Powers 46
     - Resource Transfers 47
     - An Appraisal 48
   - (IV) Fiscal Federalism in USA, Canada, Australia and Developing Nations 50

Separation in U.S.A. 50
Tax-sharing in U.S.A. 51
Grants-in-Aid in U.S.A 51
Federal Finance in Canada 53
Separation in Canada 53
Tax-Sharing in Canada 54
Grants-in-Aid in Canada 54
Federal Finance in Australia 57
Separation in Australia 57
Tax-Sharing in Australia 58
Grants-in-Aid in Australia 59
Federal Finance in Underdeveloped Countries 60
(V) Financial Agreements in Developing Countries: 63
(a) Customs and Excise Duties 64
(b) Income Tax 64
(c) Federal Grants to States 65
(d) The Government Borrowing 66
(e) Emergency Provisions 67
(f) Inter-Governmental Financial Institutions 67
(g) Recent Trends 70

**3. CHANNELS OF UNION-STATE TRANSFERS IN INDIA 71**
(I) Need of Transfer of Resources 71
(II) Channel of Transfer 71
Statutory Sources: 72
(i) Sharing of Income Tax in India 73
(ii) Sharing of Union Excise Duties 81
(iii) Sharing of Additional Duties of Excise 91
(iv) Grants-in-Aid in Lieu of Jute Export Duty 98
(v) Distribution of Estate Duty 99
(vi) Distri' ution of Tax on Railway Passenger Fares 102
(vii) Grant on Account of Wealth Tax on Agricultural Property 105
(viii) Grants-in-Aid in India 106
The Role of Grants-in-Aid 108
Distribution of Grants-in-aid in India 111
Transfer for Resources through Finance Commission in India 120
(III) Finance Commission and Planning Commission 124
The Duration of Finance Commission and the Presidents 124

Comparison of Ninth and Tenth Finance Commission 129
The Problem of Co-ordination Between Finance Commission and Planning Commission in India 129
Demarcation of the Functions of Planning Commission and Finance Commission 133

**4. UNION-STATE CONFLICTS 136**
CENTRE-STATE CONFLICTS ON FINANCES: 136
Responsibility and Resources of the Centre and of the States 137
Sources of Conflict Listed by the States 138
States Complaint on Financial Arrangements 139
Regional Imbalances as a Source of Conflict 141
The States' Demand 141
The Centre's Case 142
PROBLEMS OF LESS DEVELOPED STATE IN INDIA: 144
The Question of State Autonomy 145
Reduced Importance of Finance Commission 146
Failure to Tackle the Problem of Regional Imbalance to any Satisfactory Extent 146
SARKARIA COMMISSION: 147
View Point of the States 147
Viewpoint of the Union 151

**5. SUMMARY, CONCLUSION AND RECOMMENDATIONS 165**

Appendices 172

Bibliography 179

Index 182

# Preface

Understanding the economic structure of India is the only key which can assist the government and non-government organizations in taking a critical economic decision. Without a full fledged, fundamental and proper knowledge of the economic policies of the country, any step that is taken for the growth and development would be mere a stone thrown in the moving river water. There would be no greater positive impact, it may rather sometimes result in the negative effects as well. So, an eagle's eye need to be regularly monitoring the economic moves taken by the government.

In this book "Fiscal Federalism in India", emphasis has been given on making the minds aware of the Concept of Fiscal Federalism, Union-State Fiscal Relation in India, Channels of Union-State Transfers in India, and Union-State Conflicts. Union-states fiscal relations have been subject of study of the quinquennial finance commission and of the planning commission of India. Several social scientists, political thinkers and Economists have time to time in their studies suggested ways and means to improve these relations. However, these are live problems even today which emphasize the need for corrective measures and that justifies the study.

This book gives a detailed picture of fiscal element starting from the basics to the complex interactions in Fiscal federalism in India. In this study the balancing dimensions of union-state fiscal relations has been taken into account and such measures has been suggested which is necessary for the balanced growth of all the regions because balanced growth is National Objective of Indian Planning. It is important in academic as well as in public interest.

DR. KUMARI REKHA

# 1

# *Concept of Fiscal Federalism*

## (I) POLITICAL BASE OF FISCAL FEDERALISM

Article 1 of the Indian Constitution states, that India is a Union of States. It is a federal country; there are criticisms that it is a unitary or quasi-federal state and much of this criticism stems from the functioning of centre-state fiscal/financial relations.

Fiscal federalism is a specialized subject and comes under the study of public economics and administration. It is concerned with understanding which functions and instruments are best centralized and are best placed in the sphere of decentralized levels of government. It deals with allocation of competencies (expenditure side) and fiscal instruments (revenue side) across different layers of the administration.

The concept applies to all forms of government: unitary, federal and co-federal. It is associated with fiscal decentralization as fiscal federalism is in general a normative framework for assignment of functions to different levels of government, and appropriate fiscal instruments to carry out those functions. In other words, it is a dynamic concept and talks about "what it is" as well as "what it ought to be".

Intrinsically, the concept is related to the performance of the public sector (and its improvement), and the provision of their services by ensuring a proper alignment of their (different layers of the administration) responsibilities and fiscal instruments. Economic efficiency in the delivery of public services and welfare maximization should be the guiding principle of an optimal division of jurisdictional authority. In short, fiscal federalism is linked with fiscal decentralization.

Other than the impact of globalization and deepening of democracy, the reasons for greater fiscal federalism are as follows:

(a) central government is finding that it is impossible for them to meet all of the competing needs of various constituencies, and are attempting to build local capacity by delegating responsibilities to their sub-national governments;
(b) central government is dependent on sub-national governments to assist them on national economic development strategies; and
(c) sub-national political leaders are demanding more autonomy and want the taxation powers that go along with their expenditure responsibility.

The theoretical framework of fiscal federalism is based on the identified roles for the government/public sector. They are as follows:

I. correcting various forms of market failure,
II. ensuring an equitable distribution of income between different jurisdictions, and
III. seeking to maintain macro-economic stability at full employment and stable prices.

Federalism is today one of the most widespread principles of political organization. Federal system were at least nominally operative in 17 countries in 1981, and at least 18 others utilize federal principles to incorporate a measure of decentralization in to their system of government. Federalism is in every case, a means of organizing power and the relationships that flow it most particularly, it is a means for sharing power in political and social systems. Conceived in the broadest sense, federalism looks to the linkage of people and institution in lasting yet limited union by mutual consent, without the sacrifice of their respective integrities, as the ideal form of social or political organization.

As a basis of political association, federalism may be defined as the mode of political organization that under separate politics within an overarching political system in such a way as to allow each to maintain its own fundamental political integrity. Federal systems do this by requiring that basic policies be made implemented through negotiation in some form, so that all the members can share in-making and executing decision. The political principles that animate federal system emphasize the primacy of bargaining and negotiated coordination among several power centres, they search the virtues of dispersed power centres as a means for safeguarding individual and local liberties.

The very terminology of federalism is characterized by a revealing ambiguity. The verb federalism is used to describe the unification of separate states in to a federal policy and also the permanent diffusion of authority and power within a nation among general and sub-national governments. In this ambiguity lies the essence of the federal principle; the perpetuation of both union and non-centralization.

Federalism is more that simply a structural arrangement; it is a special mode of political and social behavior as well, involving a commitment to partnership and to active cooperation on the part of individuals and institution that at the same time take pride in preserving their own respective integrities.

A.H. Birch opines, "A federal system of government is one in which there is a division of powers between one general and several regional authorities each of which in its own sphere, is co-ordinate with the other and each of which acts directly on the people through its own administrative agencies".[1]

## History of Feseralism and the Federal Idea

Federal institutions have developed in response to two different situations. On the one hand, federalism has been used as a means to unite a people already linked by bonds of perceived nationality or by common law; in such cases, the polities that constitute the federal system are inalterably parts of the national whole, and federalism invariably leads to the development of a strong national government operating in direct contact with the people, just as the constituent governments do. The United States is a good example of this form.

On the other hand, federalism has been used as a means to unify separate peoples for important but limited purposes, leaving the individual polities a considerable degree of autonomy. Yugoslavia is one example of this form.

### *Precursors and Prototypes*

The principles of strong national federalism were first applied by the ancient Israelites, beginning in the 13th century BC, to maintain their national unity by linking their several tribes. The record of and rationale for their effort is presented in the Bible, particularly in the Books of Joshua, Judges, Samuel, and Ezekiel. It was to have a profound influence on the political principles of later generation, particularly at the time of the revival of federal ideas in the 16th and 17th centuries.

The Greek cities experimented with federal-style institutions as means for the promotion of intercity harmony and cooperation primarily for defensive purposes, through such associations as the Achaean League (280-146 BC). These came close are today defined as confederations. But Greek political philosophers ignored federalism as a political principle, because the very idea contradicted their conception of the small, unified polis as the basis of the good society. A modified form of the Greek view was developed by the 16th century theorists of international law, who held that a federation could be no more than a permanent league of states that delegated limited powers to a common governing council while retaining full internal sovereignty.

When the American federal system was created in the late 18th century, its architects developed a conception of federalism much like that of ancient Israel, a conception already rooted in American soil as a result of earlier experiments. American federalism was adapted to serve a people with a single national identity who desired a strong national government. In advocating ratification of the constitution, the authors of the federalist felt it necessary to describe the system as "partly national and partly federal" in difference to the accepted view. But in their usage the term federalist soon came to mean the older conception of federalism as a non-centralized national union having a general government superior to the governments of the constituent states.

As the American system became the prototype for other modern federal systems, the American conception of federalism became the generally accepted one in the modern world. The other conception deriving from the Greek experience came to be called confederation. These different terms correspond roughly to the German term developed in the mid-19th century: **Staatenbund** ("confederation") and **Bundesstaat** ("federation"). In French and Spanish, however, the meaning of the terms is often reversed.

Through the American conception of federalism as a strong national union confederation remains a living and legitimate aspect of the federal idea in the largest political union (the European Economic Community, or common market, is co federally organized) and by many "world federalists".

### *Cultural Home Rule and Feudalism*

Two major forms of government, both of ancient origin, utilize what seem to be federal principles but actually are not.

Several great empires, notable the Persian and roman structured their political systems around a principle that may be described as cultural home rule, a pattern followed by the late Soviet Union and China. Political life was closely involved with religion and culture in the ancient world, and imperial recognition of local ways implied a measure of contractual devolution of political power. Such home rule was not a matter of local right but represented a conditional grant subject to revolution.

The political system of federalism is often seen as a manifestation of certain federal principles because of its emphasis on contractual relationships. The Holy Roman Empire came to be the exemplary embodiment of quasi-federal feudalism. The hierarchical character of those relationships, however and the lack of practical mechanisms to maintain the terms of the contract prevented them from being truly federal. The federalism of some Latin American states is a contemporary manifestation of feudal arrangements because the constituent states are often governed by local military leaders (caudillos) who resemble feudal barons.

### *The Middle Age*

More genuinely federal were the leagues of medieval commercial towns in central Europe, formed for mutual defense and assistance. In their corporate form of internal organization, these cities paralleled the Jewish Communities of Europe and the Mediterranean world that had always organized themselves on federal principles. All Jewish communities were considered partnerships in Jewish law, created by **Askamot** (article of agreement). Beginning in the 12th century, these Jewish communities frequently joined in leagues similar to those of the new non-Jewish cities.

In 1291 the Swiss cantons formed a confederation for mutual aid in defense of their independence. It has undergone several reconstitutions, the Swiss confederation remains essentially intact, and the oldest continuing federal system in the world. It succeeded partly because it was rooted in popular government from the first.

The Christian states on the Spanish peninsula created a political system that ultimately came very close to authentic federalism. During the reconquest of Spain from the Moors, most of the peninsula was reorganized under the fuero system, which established local government liberal political institutions to encourage resettlement. Three new states arose that joined in a quasi-federal arrangement under the crown of Aragon, each of them (plus several in Italy added later) retaining its own constitution and governing institutions as well as acquiring representation in the overall Aragonese government. The union of Aragon and Castille (a unitary state) under Ferdinand and Isabella undermined the evolution toward federalism in Spain.

In the 16th century, the idea of the protestant Reformation (particularly its Calvinist and Zwinglian elements) and the example of the Spanish system of political organization led to new applications of federal principles. The Habsburg heirs to the Spanish crown had applied Spanish principles to organize their other European possessions. In the Netherlands they laid an organizational basis for the subsequent federation of the united provinces in the last 16th century, influenced in part by Calvinist ideas, when the country gained its independence it established a political system that, while falling to solve the technical problems of federalism maintained itself in federal style for 200 years. Every after Napoleon put an end to the republic, a residue of non-centralization remained; The Netherlands is now a constructionally decentralized unitary states.

The Reformation gave to the development of federalism as a social principle in Switzerland, Scotland, the Netherlands, England and parts of France and Germany. The assumptions of the puritan, Presbyterian and Reformed churches were manifested, in the formation of communities of the saved; these covenanted together to create congregations (and, in some cases, states) that they could govern as partnerships. The swish and the Dutch created federal states; the Scots re-established their national identity through the Scottish national covenant and puritans organized their New England colonies and church a federal principle. The French term for the Protestants, Huguenot, was a corruption of the German Eidgennossen, which meant confederates bound together by oath.

### *Modern Approaches*

The Dutch and Swiss precedents stimulated the first serious efforts to formulation federal theories based on modern political principles. The French political philosopher Jean Bodin analyzed the possibilities of federation in the light of the problem of sovereignty, concluding that the necessity of maintaining sovereignty indivisible within states rendered federalism in the modern sense impossible, though Greek-style leagues for defensive purposes were not incompatible with national sovereignty. The Dutch jurist Hugo Grotius and the German writer Samuel Pufendorf examined federal arrangements as aspects of international law. Grotitus, with the Dutch experience before him, concluded that closely knit leagues could prove viable, but Pufendorf held that federalism and sovereignty were so incompatible as to make leagues of any kind infringements upon sovereignty.

The German jurist Johannus Althusius, analyzing the Dutch and Swiss constitutions, perceived that federalism was really concerned with problems of national unity. The first systematic theorist of federalism, he was also the first to connect federalism with popular sovereignty and to distinguish among leagues, multiple monarchies, and confederations. His retention of hierarchical principle and his corporate organization of society reflected the realities of his time.

The application of federalism to the problems unifying the new nation-states of the $16^{th}$ and $17^{th}$ centuries encountered three problems:

(1) The difficulty of reconciling a traditionally hierarchical society with the need for fundamental social equality in the sharing of power,
(2) The conflict between local autonomy and the need for a strong central government, and
(3) The problem of executive leadership and succession, which was not solved until the American federalists invented the elected presidency.

It was the British who created the requisite popular institutions in their colonization of North America and the biblically influenced colonists who established the social basis and the theoretical justification for those institutions. The Americans assumed that their relationship to the British government was federal, even though London entertained no such notion. The American's response to the imperial system lad to develop the federal ideas they were later to use so creatively.

In transforming the principles of federalism in to a practical system of government, the Americans had the advantage of working with an entirely modern, post-feudal society that was not weighted down with traditional social hierarchies having differential political rights. Being a relatively isolated nation, they escaped the foreign entanglements that create a demand for the centralization of power. Even so, the internal problems of applying the federal principle eventually led to a major civil war.

Almost every other nation attempting the federal solution to the problems of popular government in pluralistic civil societies has attempted to imitate either the forms or the principles of federal organization worked out in the United States. The theoretical framework for those principles was developed in the debate over ratification of the constitution. At its core was the classic formulation of the principles of modern federalism in the Federalist by Alexander Hamilton, John Jay and principally, the James Madison. Equally important were the arguments of the "anti-federalists", those who wished to preserve even greater state autonomy; many of their arguments remained alive and worked to promote extra constitutional decentralization in the United States during the 19th century.

The French Revolution, for its entire democratic ethos, was essentially hostile to the spirit and institutions of federalism. Jacobin democracy drew its inspiration from Rousseau's concept of the general will as interpreted by the revolutionary leadership. Unlike federal democracy, which views the constitutional sharing of power among multiple centers (non-centralization) as the keystone of popular government, Jacobin democracy is committed to centralize majority rule whereby a single elite guides the state by interpreting the general will of its citizens as seen in "public opinion"—whether expressed or manipulated. The immediate heirs of the French Revolution endeavored to destroy federal institution; western Europe in the name of democracy, and subsequent have proved equally hostile to federal ideas except in so far as some of them have equated federalism with decentralized government. The minority tradition among the French that endorsed federalism was later to emerge as an intellectual force in the works of Alexis de Tocqueville and as a political movement in the moderate Socialism of Pierre-Joseph Proudhon and Claude Henri Saint Simon.

In the 19th century, several of the new Latin American nations experimented more and less successfully with federalism. The three largest Latin American nations, Argentina, Brazil, and Mexico, retain federal system of varying political significance, as does Venezuela; federal principles are also included in the political system of Colombia and Central American common market (established in 1958). Latin America federalism however, has remained primarily a modern manifestation of feudalistic federalism, with jefes and caudillos replacing counts and dukes.

In the mid-19th century, some Europeans turned to federalism as a form of democratic political organization. They were stimulated by necessity, the American example, and the very influential studies of Tocqueville. Numerous works were written, primarily in the German speaking counties, where federal or quasi-federal solution to the problems of political integration were highly regarded and widely used. The most important of these works were the theoretical formulations of the Swiss jurist J.K. Blutschli based on his observation of federal reorganization in Switzerland, and the historical studies of the German jurist Otto von Gierke. Federal principles were used in the unification of Germany (1866-71): and Switzerland adopted a modern federal constitution. The Netherland, Sweden, Belgium, and the Austro-Hungarian Empire adopted quasi-federal institution to meet particular problems of unification and decentralization.

Later in the century, a school of British theorists and men of affairs emerged advocating the transformation of the British Empire into the imperial federation. Canada and Australia were given federal constitution and dominion status in 1867 and 1901, respectively; the foundations were laid for the federal unification of India; and an attempt to give New Zealand a federal form of government was abandoned only at the request of the New Zealanders. Theorists such as James Bryce and E. A. Freeman, interested in imperial unity and internal devolution, made their own contribution to federal theory.

Federalism was also taken up in the 19th century by ethnic groups seeking national unity and political autonomy but not in a position to achieve them in any other way. This was the case in Austria Hungary and Balkan countries. In the 20th century, federalism has been used as a means to unify multi-ethnic nations. Several of the ethnically heterogeneous nations created or reconstructed after World War I, including the Soviet Union and Yugoslavia have formally embraced federalism as a solution to their nationality problems. The British added a federal dimension to accommodate the Ulster Irish. The emergence of new independent countries in Asia and Africa where ethnic diversity is even greater than in Europe, has led to a further application of federal principles in India and Malaysia, federalism has been used to secure political and cultural rights for large ethno linguistic groups; in Africa, federalism has been applied in several nations, including Nigeria and Cameroon as a device primarily for sharing political power.

Mention should be made of certain experiments in confederation since World War II that have sought to link independent countries for mainly economic purposes; the European Economic Community, or Common Market established by Costa Rica, EI Salvador, Guatemala, Honduras, Nicaragua; and the confederation of Arab Republics comprised of Egypt, Libya and Syria.

## Federal Principles

In addition to full-fledged federal systems, there are other forms of political order that make use of certain principles; multiple monarchies, legislative unions, empires decentralized unitary systems and unions of non-territorial units.

The multiple monarchies are a union that exists only in the person of the sovereign and is maintained only through the exercise of executive power in his name. There is no common legislature, no common legal system, nor much of any common political substructure. Each constituent polity maintains its own political system, which the monarch guarantees to support.

Multiple monarchies have historically been somewhat incompatible with democratic government, and this has been a source of their instability. Attempts to transfer sovereignty away from the monarch are likely to destroy the union. Thus, the Austro-Hungarian Empire disintegrated when the Habsburgs ceased to rule. The dual monarchy of Sweden and Norway ceased to function when democratic government was introduced. In Spain, on the other hand, where circumstances required some form of peninsular union, the multiple monarchies was replaced by something approximating a unitary state.

One method for better integrating multiple monarchies, while preserving decentralized government is by legislative union. This was used in the United Kingdom, uniting England, Wales, Scotland, and Northern Ireland. The 17th century dual monarchy linking England and Scotland was stabilized through a legislative union of the nations in 1707; Legislative union resembles federal union at several crucial points. It is created by a perpetual covenant that guarantees the constituent parties their boundaries, representation in the national legislature, and certain local autonomies in such matters as municipal law. In the United Kingdom, the cabinet has acquired supremacy not foreseen in 1707; but, within the framework of cabinet government, Northern Ireland has been granted its own parliament with substantial local autonomy, Scotland has acquired a national ministry of its own with a separate administrative structure for most of its governmental programs, and Wales has gained a Welsh Office with growing administrative powers.

Some empires make limited use of federal principles through grants of cultural home rule. The Persian and Roman empires did so in the ancient world, and the U.S.S.R. may well be the modern counterpart. In both cases, highly centralized political authorities possessing a virtual monopoly of power decide, for reasons of policy, to allow local populations with different ethnic or cultural backgrounds to maintain a degree home rule provided that they remain politically loyal to the imperial regime. Efforts to transform such home rule into serious political power are invariably suppressed by the central government.

The use of federal principles also found in decentralized unitary states. These guarantee their local governments considerable autonomy in some area, limited to matters determined by the central authorities to be local, such local powers are subject to national supervision, restriction and even withdrawal. The central government may hesitate to take such action in areas where local privileges are well established, but the English experience has shown, even powerful traditions supporting local autonomy have been overridden by democratically elected parliaments with the support of a national majority.

Some apparently centralized states are actually quasi-federal unions of ethnic, religious or ideological groups that, while not organized territorially, have acquired corporate characteristic of their own and have been able to secure constitutional arrangements designed to preserve their respective integrities within a common polity. Belgium, with its linguistic communities, Lebanon, with its religious communities, Cyprus, with its ethnic communities and Israel, with its ideological parties, exemplifies this arrangement. In most of these cases, domestic services and responsibilities are shared by the sub-communities, which are responsible for serving their adherents under the general aegis of the state.

Federative and confederative arrangements are widely used

outside the governmental realm to unify or integrate religions, lobour, commercial and cultural organizations. Federative organization is particularly common in the Calvinist and Reformed churches, ranging from the fully federal Presbyterians to the loosely confederated Baptists. Labour unions and business groups are frequently functional federation. Liberal democracy, with its emphasis on pluralism, is highly conductive to such arrangements.

## Characteristics of Federal Systems

The various political systems that call themselves federal differ in many ways. Certain characteristics and principles, however, are common to all truly federal system.[2]

### *Basic Elements*

Written constitution, First, the federal relationship must be established or confirmed through a perpetual covenant of union, usually embodies in a written constitution that outlines the terms by which power is divided or shared in the political system, the constitution can be altered only by extraordinary procedures. Every existing federal policy possesses a written constitution, as do most of the other systems incorporating elements of the federal principle. These constitutions are distinctive in being not simply compacts between rulers and ruled but involving the people, the general government, and polities constituting the federal union. The constituent polities, moreover, often retain constitution-making rights of their own.

### *Non-centralization*

Second, the political system itself must reflect the constitution by actually diffusing power among a number of substantially self-sustaining centres. Such a diffusion of power may be termed non-centralization. Non-centralization is quite different from decentralization, which is the conditional diffusion of specific powers by a central government to local governments subject to recall by unilateral decision. It is also more than devolution—the unilateral grant of powers to sub-national units by a central government, not normally rescindable. Non-centralization is a way of insuring in practice that the authority to participate in exercising political power cannot be taken away from the general or the constituent governments without common consent.

### *Areal Division of Power*

A third element of any federal system is what has been called in the United States territorial democracy. This has two faces: the use of areal divisions to ensure neutrality and equality in the representation of the various groups and interests in the polity and the use of such divisions to secure local autonomy and representation for diverse groups within the same civil society. While seemingly contradictory, both faces are closely related to the purposes of federalism, and manifestations of both are frequently found side by side within the same federal system. Territorial neutrality has proved highly useful in societies that are changing, allowing for the representation of new interests in proportion to their strength by allowing their supporters to vote in relatively equal territorial units. At the same time, the accommodation of very diverse groups whose differences are fundamental rather than transient by giving them territorial power bases of their own has enhanced the ability of the federal systems to function as vehicles of political integration while preserving democratic government. Examples are Yugoslavia, where each constituent republic is organized around a different nationality group, and Canada, where the province of Quebec contains a population of French descent.

Historically, constitutionally fixed areal divisions of power have been necessary to maintain non-centralization. In modern democratic theory the argument between federalists and pluralists has frequently revolved around the respective values of areal and functional diffusions of power. Those who have argued the obsolescence of federalism while endorsing its values have generally based their case on the argument that the areal division of powers is unnecessary to preserve liberty and, indeed, may interfere with its protection. Proponents of the federal-areal division argue that the deficiencies of territorial democracy are greatly outweighed by the advantages of a guaranteed power base for each group in the political system, arguing further that any other system devised for giving them power has proved unable to cope with the complexities and changes of a dynamic age.

### *Other Elements of Federalism*

Other supportive elements supplement the three basic ones. They can be grouped according to their primary impact on the systems they serve.

#### *Elements maintaining union*

Modern federal systems generally provide direct lines of communication between the citizenry and all the governments that serve them. The people may and usually do elect representatives to all the governments, and all of them may and usually do administer programs that directly serve the individual citizen.

The existence of those direct lines of communication is one of the features distinguishing federations from leagues or confederations. It is usually based on a sense of common nationality binding the constituent polities and people together. In some countries this sense of nationality has been inherited, as is Germany, while in the United States, Argentina, Switzerland, and Yugoslavia have had to evolve this sense in order to hold together strongly divergent nationality groups in the newly formed federal systems of India, Malaysia, and Nigeria, the future of federalism is endangered by the absence of such a common national sense.

Geographic necessity has played a part in promoting the maintenance of union within federal systems. The Mississippi Valley in the United States, the Alps in Switzerland, the island character of the Australian continent, the mountains and jungles surrounding Brazil have all been influences promoting unity; so have the pressures for Canadian union arising from that country's situation on the border of the United States and the pressures upon the German states generated by their neighbors to the east and west. In this connection, the necessity for a common defense against common enemies has stimulated federal union in the first place and acted to maintain it.

### *Elements maintaining non-centralization*

The constituent polities in a federal system must be fairly equal in population and wealth or else balanced geographically pr numerically in their inequalities. In the United States, each geographic section has included both great and small states. In Canada, the ethnic differences between the two largest and richest provinces have prevented them from combining against the others. Swiss federalism has been supported by the existence of groups of cantons of different size categories and religio-linguistic backgrounds. Similar distributions exist in every other successful federal system.

A major reason for the failure of federal systems has often been a lack of balance among the constituent polities. In the German federal empire of the late 19th Century, Prussia was so dominant that the other states had little opportunity to provide national leadership or even a reasonably strong alternative to the policy of the king and government. In the Soviet Union, the existence of the Russian Soviet Federated Socialist Republic occupying three-fourths of the area and containing three-fifths of the population would severely limit the possibility of authentic federal relationships in that country even if the communist system did not.

Successful federal systems have also been characterized by the permanence of their internal boundaries. Boundary changes may occur, but such changes are made only with the consent of the polities involved and are avoided except in extreme situations. The United States divided Virginia during its civil war. Canada enlarged the boundaries of its provinces, and Switzerland has divided cantons—but these have been exceptions rather than the rule, and in every case the formal consent of the constituent polities was given. Even in Latin America, state boundaries have tended to remain relatively secure; one of the major bulwarks of Latin American federalism has been the coincidence of state boundaries with major social and economic interests or ethnic-cultural groups.

In a few very important cases, non-centralization is given support through the constitutionally guaranteed existence of different systems of law in the constituent polities. In the United States, each state's legal system stems directly and to a certain extent uniquely from English (and, in one case, French) law, while federal law occupies only an interstitial position binding the systems of the 50 states together. The resulting mixture of laws keeps the administration of justice substantially non-centralized, even in federal courts. In Canada, the existence of common-law and civil-law systems side by side has contributed to French-Canadian cultural survival. Non-centralized legal systems are a particularly Anglo-American device, based as they are on traditional common law. Federal systems more often provide for modification of national legal codes by the sub-national governments to meet special local needs, as in Switzerland.

The point has often been made that in truly federal system the constituent polities must have substantial influence over the formal or informal constitutional amending process. Since constitutional changes are often made without formal constitutional amendment, the position of the constituent polities must be such that serious changes in the political order can be made only by the decision of dispersed majorities that reflect that areal division of powers. Federal theorists have argued that this is important for popular government as well as for federalism.

Non-centralization is also strengthened by giving the constituent polities guaranteed representation in the national legislature and often by giving them a guaranteed role in the national political process. The latter is guaranteed in the written constitutions of the United States and Switzerland. In other systems, such as those of Canada and Latin America, the constituent polities have acquired certain powers of participation, and these have become part of the unwritten constitution.

Perhaps the most important single element in the maintenance of federal non-centralization is the existence of a non-centralized party system. Non-centralized parties initially develop out of the constitutional arrangements of the federal compact, but once they have come into existence they tend to be self-perpetuating and to function as decentralizing forces in their own right. The United States and Canada provide examples of the forms that a non-centralized party system may take. In the two party system of the United States, the parties actually coalitions of the state parties (which may in turn be dominated by specific local party organizations) and function as national units only for the quadrennial presidential elections or for purposes of organizing the national congress. Party financing and decision-making are dispersed either among the state organizations or among which divergent nationwide factions.

In Canada, on the other hand, the parliamentary form of government, with its requirements of party responsibility, means that on the national plane considerably more party cohesiveness must be maintained simply in order to gain and hold power. There has been a fragmentation of the parties along regional or provincial line. The one or two parties that function on a nationalized basis are subject to great shifts in popular support from one election to another. They are also divided intentionally along provincial lines, each provincial organization being more or less autonomous; at the same time, individual provinces are frequently dominated by parties that send only a few representatives to the national legislature. The victorious in national elections is likely to be the enable to expand its provincial electoral bases temporarily to nation proportions.

Federal nations with less developed party systems frequently gain some of the same decentralizing effects through what the Latin Americans call Caudillismo—in which power is diffused among strong local leaders operating in the constituent polities. Caudillistic non-centralization apparently exists also in Nigeria and Malaysia.

Ultimately, however, non-centralization is maintained through respect for the federal principle. Such respect requires recognition by the decision-making publics that the preservation of the constituent polities is as important as the preservation of the nation as a whole. As the American Chief Justice Salmon P. Chase said, federalism took to "an indestructible union, composed of indestructible states" (Texas *v.* White [1869]) This recognition may spring from loyalty to particular polities or from an understanding of the way federalism functions. Those who value a politics of conciliation and local autonomy are most likely to have respect for the federal principle.

The historical record indicates that federal systems have arisen out of the dual purpose implied in Chase's dictum at least as often as from a desire for political unification. The Canadian confederation was formed not only to make the British North American colonies but also to give Ontario and Quebec autonomous political systems. Similarly, a guiding purpose in the evolution of the Swiss confederation has been to preserve the independence of the cantons both from outside encroachment and from revolutionary centralism. A good case can be made that similar motivations also played a part in the creation of most other federal systems.

### *Elements maintaining the federal principle*

Several of the devices commonly found in federal systems serve to maintain the federal principle itself. Two of these are of particular importance.

The maintenance of federalism requires that the nation and in constituent polities each have substantially complete governing institutions of their own, with the right to modify those institutions unilaterally within limits set by the compact. Both separate legislative and separate administrative institutions are necessary. This does not require that all governmental activities be carried out by separate institutions on each plane. The agencies of one Government may serve as agents of the other by mutual agreement. But each government must have enough of its two institutions to function in the areas of its authority without depending upon the other and the structural wherewithal to cooperate freely with the other's counterpart agencies.

The contractual sharing of public responsibilities by all governments in the systems appears to be a central characteristic of federalism. Sharing, broadly conceived, includes common involvement in policy-making, financing, and administration. Sharing may be formal or informal; in federal systems, it usually contractual. The contract is used as a legal device to enable governments to engage in joint action while remaining independent entities. Even where there is no formal arrangement, the spirit of federalism tends to infuse a sense of contractual obligation.

There is likely to be continued tension in any federal system between the federal government and the constituent polities over the years, with different balances between them at different times. The existence of this tension is an integral part of the federal relationship. The questions of inter-governmental relations that it produces are perennially a matter of public concern, because they are reflected in virtually every political issue that arises. This is particularly true of those issues that affect the fabric of society. The race question in the United States, for example, is a problem of federal-state relation as is the cultural question in Canada and the linguistic question in India.

Federal systems or systems strongly influenced by federal principles have been among the most stable and long of polities. But the successful operation of federal makes conductive to popular government and has the requisite traditions of political cooperation and self-restraint. Beyond this, federal systems operate best in societies with sufficient homogeneity of fundamental interests to allow a great deal of latitude to local government and to permit reliance upon voluntary collaboration. The use of force to maintain domestic order is even more inimical to the successful maintenance of federal patterns of government than to other forms of popular government. Federal systems are most successful in societies that have the human resources to fill many public offices competently and the material resources to afford a measure of economic waste as part of the price of liberty.

## (II) NATURE OF THE INDIAN FEDERAL SYSTEM

The constitution says; "India shall be a union of States" (Art. 1) The term 'Union' was used to indicate: (a) that the Indian Federation is not the result of an agreement by the units, and (b) that the component units have no freedom to secede from. However, the term 'union' does not in itself indicate any particular type of federation. Actually, there is no agreed definition of a federal state. India's constitutional system is basically federal, but with striking unitary features.

The Indian Constitution satisfies the following characteristics of basically federal constitution:

(1) Unlike a unitary state, which has only one government, namely, the Union Government India has two kinds of governments functioning at two different levels—Union government and the government of each component state.

(2) The constitution of the states has been given by a duly constituted body consisting of the representatives of the Indian people who have made a clear cut distribution of power between the federal government and the state government.

(3) The supremacy lies with the constitution from which both the union and the state governments derive their authority. The Supreme Court has been entrusted with the responsibility of guarding the distribution of power between the centre and the states, and to invalidate any action which violates the limitations imposed by the constitution.

Peculiar Features of Indian Federalism: Unitary Aspect. The government of the country, till the Indian Act of 1935 as passed, was a centralized government and the process that was adopted under the Indian Act of 1935 was that of "creating autonomous units and combining them into a federation by one and the same Act. The process for the establishment of a federation in India has to be described as one of movement from the union to the units rather than from the units to the union.

A partition of the country, with the seceding part nurturing a grouse against it and the uncertainties of the international situation—the emergence of two super powers for supremacy over each other made it necessary for the Indian Constitution to make provision for the centralization of power. Thus, it has the following features:

(1) The residuary powers under the Indian Constitution are assigned to the Union and not to the States.
(2) The Indian Constitution lays down in considerable detail the Constitution for the States also.
(3) Except in a few specified matters affecting the federal structure, the states need not even be consulted in the matter of amendment of the Constitution.
(4) The Indian Constitution provides the Union with power to exercise control over the legislation as well as the administration of the state sphere in possible only the consent of the Council of States. The Union Government can issue directions upon the state Governments to ensure due compliance with the legislative and administrative action of the Union. The President can withdraw to the Union the executive and legislative powers of a state under the Constitution if he is, at any time, satisfied that the administration of the state cannot be carried on in the normal manner in accordance with the provisions of the Constitution, owing to political or other reasons. A legislation by a state can be reserved by the Governor for his consideration and disallowed by the President, if he so decides.
(5) In the case of Indian Constitution, while the Union is indestructible the States are not. It is possible for the Union Parliament to reorganize the States or to alter their boundaries by a simple majority in the ordinary process of legislation.
(6) There is only a citizenship, namely, The Citizenship of India.
(7) The constitution itself provides for certain All India Services, which are common in between the Union and the States.
(8) India has a unified Judiciary, which administers both the Union and State laws as might be applicable to the cases coming up for adjudication. Also in matters of election, as well as in accounts and audit, there is similar integrated machinery.

Some scholars have urged that the unitary bias of our

Constitution has been accentuated, in the actual working by two factors so much so that very little is left of federalism. These two factors are:

(a) The overwhelming financial power of the Union and the utter dependence of the States upon Union grants for discharging their functions, and

(b) The comprehensive sweep of the Union Planning Commission.

However, both these controls are aimed at securing a uniform development of the country as a whole.

*A Compromise:*

In fact, the federal systems in the Indian Constitution in a compromise between two apparently conflicting considerations:

(i) There is a normal division of power under which the States enjoy autonomy within their own sphere, with the power to raise revenue, and

(ii) The need for national integrity and a strong Union government, which the saner section of the people still consider necessary after 40 years of working of the Constitution.[3]

## (III) ECONOMIC INTERPRETATION OF FEDERALISM

Under federal system responsibilities are fixed between the Union and the States. Adequate finance is required to meet the responsibilities. If the states are debarred from financial power their administrative and legislative relations would be deemed. In this regard Dr. D.D. Basu remarked:

> "No system of federalism can be successful unless both the union and the states have their disposal adequate financial resources to enable them to discharge their respective responsibilities under the constitution."[4]

The Supreme Court, in their verdict on Coffee Board C.T.O., remarked:

> "Sources of revenue which have been allocated to the Union are not meant entirely for the purpose of the union but have to be distributed according to the principles laid down by the parliamentary legislation as contemplated by the Article aforesaid.

Thus all the taxes and duties levied by the union do not form part of Consolidated Fund of India but many of these taxes and duties are distributed among the states and form part of the Consolidated Fund of the States. Even those taxes and duties which constitute the Consolidated Fund of India may be used for the purpose of supplementing the revenues of the states in accordance with their needs.

Realizing the limitations of the financial resources and the growing needs of the community in welfare states, the constitution has made specific provisions empowering parliament to set aside a portion of its revenue for the benefit of the states, not in stated proportions but according to their needs." [5]

The federal principle of financial autonomy had never been applied in total. In Canada and Australia the states have very meager source of revenue to meet the requirement. In Switzerland, on the contrary, union is dependent on the states for finance. In U.S.A., there has been a tendency to balance the sources of income between the union and the states, yet the states are bound to receive grant, from centre. The same problem lies in India. The states have limited resources of revenue to discharge their responsibilities.

## (IV) BARGAINING PROCESS UNDER FEDERAL SET-UP

The policies of a federal set-up are a product not only of the bargaining which takes place between the central and unit government but also of the bargaining among the unit governments. The extent of the bargaining which takes place amongst the governments in a federal set-up will depend upon the degree in which the decisions of government affect one another and the extent to which government's electorates make demands which cannot be satisfied by the governments without securing a modification of other government policies or a change in the division of decision-making powers between the central and unit governments. The nature of the bargaining process will depend mainly on the power potentials of the various governments, the rules of the game embodied in the constitution and bargaining capabilities.[6]

In many respects the process of bargaining between governments in a federal system is similar to that of nations in international politics. However, there is one major difference which follows from the dual nature of the federal government and Coincidence of electorates that we can never wholly separate national politics and central government interests from unit politics and interest of units. In other words, every federal system displays also some of the characteristics of a unitary state.

In the federal system, the central government occupies a peculiar dual role in the bargaining process. First, it is the government representing the nation and is responsible to its own national electorate. As such it exists as an independent entity in the bargaining process and participates, with the unit government, in the competition for satisfying the demands of its electorate. Secondly, since the nation is the aggregate of the unites which comprise it, the central government's electorate, the members of the central parliament, the political parties and pressure groups which participate in national politics, and the bureaucrats serving in the central administration, all will project, on to the central government, political demands and attitudes which arise within the units. In such a situation the central government will serve as a receptacle for the interaction of unit interests. In other words, the interests of the central governments are the netting of interests arising within units. Because of its position as Government for the nation as a whole, many a time it has to play the third role of acting as a mediator and referee—through inevitably not an 'objective' referee-in the conflicts of interests between the unit governments.

The initial federal agreement, as embodied in the federal constitution, generally provides the starting point for bargaining. The constitution of federal system represents the original compromise of interests between the members of the federation with regard to both the expected gains from the federation and the rules governing future bargaining and negotiations. The process of drawing up a federal constitution is most interesting in those countries where a number of existing states decide to come together to form a federation because of interplay of political forces. However, the basic problem in drawing up a federal constitution to achieve a compromise in such a way that the states in a strong bargaining position expects to make sufficient gains from the membership of the federation worth-while. At the same time, they do not press their advantage to point where states with weaker bargaining power have no inducement to join. The fundamental process of federating, therefore, is guided by dual instincts of self-interest and mutual adjustment. Each federating unit, therefore, while largely safeguarding its own interest reaches out beyond itself to contribute to a larger interest which comprises the interests of all the federating units, and hence its philosophy basically is that of accommodation, mutuality and a larger comprehension of regional and national needs and interests. However, there is another kind of federation of which India is a significant example. Such federations are formed by political exigencies through the process of disintegration of an existing state. But for the future stability of the federation the basic problem is the same. As such there must be some sort of balance established between the interests of units.

The effect of federation is not just to create a new bargaining arena within which units of the federation compete and cooperate with one another. The act of federation results in a transformation of the units themselves. There are two elements in this transformation; the first results from the fact that the units transfer some jurisdiction to the central government, over which no unit government has control, and the second results from the fact that each unit becomes a component of the national whole and interests within the unit are reoriented so to take account of the new national forces to which they are subject.

When countries come together in an economic union, two important adjustments take place. First, with the removal of tariffs and other barriers to trade there will be a realignment of trade between the members of the union and countries outside the union. Thus, there will be a wide range of possible outcome of trade realignment, which the theory of customs unions has sought to systematize. Secondly, there will be shift in the factor of production. With the breaking down of national frontiers, labour and capital are more likely to move to those fields in which their returns are the highest. There is no doubt that it will result in a larger benefit to the union as a whole. However, there is little evidence to suggest that this is the general case. On the contrary, there is substantial agreement that economic integration is likely, for a while at least, to increase rather than reduce economic inequalities between regions. In the United States the development of a nation economy, with a realignment of trade, and the territorial expansion of the federation intensified the clash of economic interests between the Northern and Southern States; the fear by the south of permanent economic inferiority within the federation was a reason for its move to secede. In Canada and Australia too, the smaller, predominantly primary producing units had reservations about the effects on prices of trade diversion and on local industry of the competition which economic integration would bring from the larger, more industrially advanced units. Among the newer federations, in the West Indies not only did some of the potential members of federation abstain partly for economic reasons but when the federation was set-up, there was no customs union, there were restrictions on the freedom of movement of population, and the economic powers of the central government were severely limited. In Malaysia also, Sarawak and Sabah secured the right to control inter-state migration and Singapore was not prepared to join the federation without being assured of its status as a free port and its autonomy in certain fields, including labour policy.

There is no denying the fact that the tendency to limit integration or to promote it will largely depend on inequalities among the units and the likely distribution of gains from economic integration. When the units which stand to gain most from integration are large and wealthy, federal policy is likely to promote integration, though the small poor units may raise objections. Where the units which stand to gain most are large but not relatively wealthy; federation is likely to be unstable because the relatively wealthy small units may have little economic incentive to federate. Where the gain goes to small wealthy units, again the federation may be unstable. Finally, where the gain goes to small poor units the crucial factor will be whether the large wealthy units are prepared to give up something of their relative economic superiority out of generosity or other reasons. In all these cases if the units which stand to gain can compensate those which stand to lose the chances of securing full integration are greater.

## (V) PROBLEM OF FISCAL ADJUSTMENTS

The federal form of government is constituted with a hope that such a government will be efficient for the nation as a whole. Subjects of common interest are assigned to the central government and those which are of local or regional interests are assigned to the unit governments. Like the division of functions between the central and unit governments, the division of resources are also based on the principle of relative interest and efficiency. Taxes which have inter-state base, like customs, income and wealth tax, are assigned to the federal government and those which have a local base like sales tax and entertainment tax are assigned to the units.

In most of the federations the allocation of customs and exise to the central government has left units without a major source of revenue and has given the central government initially a surplus over its immediate needs. Also the central government's superiority in revenue raising has been strengthened by its movement into the field of income taxation. In such a situation a transfer of revenue from the central to unit governments has been necessary to enable the unit governments to carry out the functions assigned to them. In this context, the role of fiscal adjustment between governments in federal systems becomes more important.

There are two broad sets of reasons for such a transfer; the first arising from the transfer of jurisdiction to a second level of government and the second arising from the effects of national orientation.

There is no doubt that the federation will create demands for national standards, including the provision of public services; and the poorer units may be unable to afford the higher level of expenditure demanded. This will necessarily create a demand for a redistribution of public revenue in favor of the poorer states. There is no doubt that some redistribution can be achieved through the regional allocation of central government's expenditure. However, in most federations the altering political situations and pressures of the poorer units have made it necessary to provide direct grants to the governments of the poorer units. Also if in the opinion of the central government a unit government is failing to give high priority to specified purposes in the national interest it may make grants to the units. In a federation some units may be worse-off, or believed to be worse-off, as a result of federation, because of the effects of economic integration and because of loss of decision-making powers in certain areas. Some of the problems of such units can be compensated in financial terms and this is perhaps yet another reason for the transfer of revenue to certain units from the central government.

The function of fiscal transfers is to allocate revenue, given the distribution of governmental functions, so as to achieve the greatest satisfaction of all governments. This implies a redistribution of income among units in such a way that the benefits to small and poor units are sufficient to maintain their interest in the federation, while the sacrifice of revenue by big and rich units is not considered by them to be greater than the benefits accruing from the federation. If a satisfactory allocation cannot be achieved, the chances of a federation surviving without internal conflicts and external pressure are slight.[7]

## (VI) GUIDING PRINCIPLES OF FISCAL ADJUSTMENTS

In all federations an attempt has been made to divide the financial resources and obligations so as to correspond to the division of the powers and functions between the central government and unit governments. By and large, earnest efforts have been made to make each unit government as well as the central government financially self-sufficient to the extent possible. However, in practice, such division is seldom perfect so as to make the resources and obligations absolutely exclusive for each level of government. Therefore, links have had to be devised which, without violating the basic principle of federal finance, would nevertheless secure adequate and just resources to each unit of a federal system.

M.V. Pylee has rightly summarized the guiding principles of federalism in the following words: "The basic principles that quote the allocation of resources between the federation and the units are efficiency, adequacy and suitability. It is indeed difficult to achieve all the three ends at the same time. Constitutional, natural and economic considerations often stand in the way. Even if a certain system might suggest itself as the most acceptable, it would not certify the claims and counter-claims of various states. Hence, the constitution has attempted a compromise. According to this, the subject is divided into two parts, namely:

(1) The allocation of revenues between the union and the states.

(2) The distribution of grants-in-aid."[8]

## (VII) FEDERAL INTER-REGIONAL TRANSFERENCE OF RESOURCES AND ECONOMIC DEVELOPMENT

At different times scholars have put forward the different principles regarding the inter-regional transference of resources which promote economic development of the country.

Was the first economist to emphasis that the division of resources should be based upon the principles of efficiency, suitability and adequacy? Dr. Gyan Chand has added integrity to this list. Prof. Adarkar has mentioned three essential features which should be satisfied for an efficient working of the federal financial system, namely, independence and responsibility, adequacy and clasticity and administrative economy. The different layers of government must have considerable freedom and initiative to raise revenue though in national interest there may be a certain measure of co-ordination and control of federal government. The resources assigned to each unit should be adequate to meet its immediate and initial needs and should be capable of expansion with its growing needs and emergencies such as war, natural calamities and depression. The assignment of resources should be so that proper balance between direct and indirect taxes as maintained to achieve equity in taxation for the nation as a whole. By administrative economy is meant that the scheme of allocation should prevent opportunities of fraud and evasion and should avoid double and multiple taxations. The cost of collection should be low. The division of resources should also be based on the principle of efficiency. Taxes with inter-state base such as customs should be administered by the states. There are many taxes which do not fall into either of these categories exclusively such as motor vehicles tax. In the Indian Constitution the principle on which taxes of such vehicles are to be levied is a subject of concurrent jurisdiction though the administration of the tax is entrusted to the states. In case of overlapping jurisdiction it is generally desirable to have federal control but the proceeds should be assigned to the states. The scheme of division of resources must ensure according to the principle of integrity that one state is not given the authority to tax the people of other states. The scheme of division of resources must set-up a clastic system of finance which may adjust with growing needs and changing economic, social, political and technological conditions. Finally, it may be desirable to have some broad federal supervision or federal advice to ensure that each state follows the principles of public finance, taxation and public expenditure and stand in line with the national fiscal policy. Some authors suggest principles such as uniformity, independence, suitability, non-discrimination, elasticity, minimum tax competition and tax conflicts and counter-cyclical adjustment of tax rates which should guide the inter-governmental fiscal relations in a federation. It may be noted that the division of resources in most federations is based upon historical reasons. Expediency rather than any adherence to scientific principles of federal finance was often the main consideration". These principles were not fully developed at the time when the older federations came into existence. In their case the only possibility is to reform the original division. The principles of federal finance are given effect to in different federation, through the separation of revenue, grants-in-aid and tax devices of sharing.[9]

In the first place, the federal government must have the constitutional authority to tax all the citizens and must have the power to levy direct taxes which can be closely related to ability, so that it can evolve a scheme of taxation in accordance with the principle of taxation. It is also essential that the federal government should have the authority to levy some indirect taxes, such as customs and excise duties so that its scheme of taxation could be made not only progressive but also comprehensive and regulatory to internal economy and international trade.

In the second place, the constitution should provide a scheme of grants-in-aid so that the federal government can make up the deficiencies of the power states and follow the principle of public expenditure for the federation as a whole. The grants should be so distributed that they ensure financial responsibility on the part of the state governments without impairing state autonomy. A system of grants ensures not only "budgetary equilibrium" for the poorer states by making their resources equal to their needs but would also ensure "economic equilibrium" for the nation as a whole. It should also promote balanced regional growth and the economic, social and political stability of the federation because "poverty anywhere is a danger to prosperity ever where."

In the third place, the division of functions and resources between the federal and the State Governments can be based on the principle of efficiency and economy. Ordinarily such a scheme of division left too few resources with the states because due to ramifications of big business, the integration of economic life and the importance of international trade, the more productive sources with as taxes on income and inheritance customs and excise duties are more efficiently administered by the federal government. On the other hand, the emergence of Welfare State necessitates expanding expenditures on social services which have to be organized on a state basis in the interest of economy and efficiency and to allow for diversities between the different regions. These discrepancies may be coped with the system of grants. However, in order to ensure fiscal autonomy to the states, it is desirable that there may be a scheme of shared taxes. The constitution may declare important taxes as "shared taxes" and also allocate a certain minimum percentage of the revenue as the state's share which can be increased through federal legislation. The federal power to increase the states quota will introduce elasticity into the system and its power to determine the separate share of different states will enable it to follow the principle of public finance for the nation as a whole. The above discussions suggest that the inter-governmental relations must be based on the principle of separation of revenue, grants-in aid and tax sharing.[10]

## (VIII) FEDERAL FINANCE AND ECONOMIC DEVELOPMENT

Besides the classical federations of U.S.A., Canada, Australia, West Germany and Switzerland, the new underdeveloped states like India, Pakistan, Malaysia, Nigeria, Central Africa and the West Indies have adopted federal forms of government. Federalism is a political device which is adopted to further ends which are always party and sometimes predominantly economic. The economic motive is more predominant in underdeveloped countries. In an underdeveloped economy, we find, low per capita real income, capital deficiency, high or low man-land ratio, vast unutilized natural resources, economic, technological, political and cultural backwardness. In such countries, as Hicks has pointed out,—"the economic development of a country is a major responsibility of its government, in particular, that if a country feels itself to be backward or underdeveloped; it is the duty of the government to cause it to "catch up". The role of federal finance in such countries is mainly to promote economic growth by accelerating the rate of saving and investment to achieve "utility optimum" and "production optimum". This implies the correction of inter-personal and inter-regional disparities in wealth and income and maximization of economic growth by accelerating output, employment and economic welfare of the nation. Federal finance has to play a positive and dynamic role for the promotion and acceleration of economic development in the underdeveloped countries and to encourage a policy of "big push". Viewed in this light, we may analysis the various objectives of federal finance in underdeveloped countries.

The first objective of federal finance in an underdeveloped country is to attain revenue sufficiency or financial adequacy. The federal government must have control of sufficient funds to perform its fundamental duties of external relations and of internal socio-economic policy. The federal government must find funds to extend financial assistance to the federating states and to finance the development plans, both at the centre and state levels. In underdeveloped countries, the rate of saving is very low and therefore the federal and state governments by its devices of "forced savings" may accentuate the rate of investment to secure maximum economic growth. Federal finance must raise adequate resources through taxation, surpluses from public enterprises and internal and external borrowing and deficit financing to attain financial adequacy both for the centre and the states. While mobilizing resources the government should also consider the economic effects of financial operations and should be guided by the principle of maximum social advantage as advocated by Dalton, Pigou, Musgrave and others.

The second objective of federal finance is the maximization of the growth rate of economy of the country as a whole by so arranging the financial relationship that each unit could exploit the growth potential to maximum possible extent and the nation as a whole may march ahead. Fiscal policy in a federal structure as an instrument of economic development is essentially concerned with effecting transfer of resources from a line having lower marginal productivity to one having a higher one. Therefore, the transfer of resources from a high income state to a low income one will be compatible with the criteria of economic growth only if such a transfer results in a higher, marginal productivity of the transferred resources. Thus the objective of fiscal policy may be to attain production optimum as emphasized by U.K. Hicks. The condition of production optimum is attained when the allocation of productive factors in the economy confirms, to the principle of equi-marginal productivity; and when the productive factors are fully and continuously employed. Fiscal policy as an effective instrument of economic planning in a federal system can make an important contribution to the achievement of production optimum by regulating the flow of productive resources and by removing the hindrances in the way of the most efficient allocation of these resources such as the monopolistic control of markets and the existence of inadequate environmental services and basic overheads. Keynes, Hansen, Kurihara, Pigou, Baveridge, Kalecki, Lerner and others supported the role of fiscal policy as a compensatory instrument in the economy contributing to the achievement of production by enabling the maintenance of full employment.

Federal finance for promoting the economic development of underdeveloped countries may have four important dimensions. viz., (i) to promote and accelerate the growth of productive investment in the economy both in the public and private sectors; (ii) to mobilize the maximum volume of real and financial resources for the investment plan of the public sector and for this to promote the growth of marginal and average rate of savings in the economy; (iii) to promote the maintenance of a reasonable measure of economic stability in keeping with the maximum rate of growth of the economy, and (iv) to re-distribute the growing national output among the individuals and different regions of the federation. Thus, the role of fiscal operations of the government for promoting the economic growth of the under-developed countries is as an investor, as a saver, as a stabilizer and as an income re-distributer.

United Nations has also supported these objectives of fiscal policy in general. According to the report of the sub-commission appointed by the United Nations the fiscal policy should correct excessive or harmful inequalities in the distribution of income and wealth and in doing so, to expand internal markets and reduce unessential imports. It should counteract the inflation which might result from economic development. The growth-oriented fiscal policy should provide incentive for desirable types of development projects and thus help to steer development into desirable directions and lastly should increase the total savings available for economic development.

The third objective of federal finance in a developing economy is to afford to each state proper and adequate opportunities for attaining a level of development which would not fall far below the general national level and bringing to the extent possible, the comparatively backward states to an average level so that the disparity amongst the state, in the matter of development and social progress could be minimized. The theoretical case for inter-regional transference of resources is based, firstly, on the concept of utility optimum as advocated by U.K. Hicks. Fiscal policy can make a contribution to the maximization of aggregate utility by redistribution of income in the community. This view of public finance involves the problem of inter-personal comparison of utility and cardinal measurability of utility which is not possible as pointed out by Pareto, Hicks, Allen and Slutsky. Besides, redistributive fiscal policy, if carried beyond a certain limit, might conflict with the objective of promoting economic growth and aggregate output in an economy. In a federal structure where centre and states follow the independent fiscal policy, the, utilitarian view of public finance is more difficult to apply. Thus it would be extremely difficult, if not impossible, to translate the theoretical implications of utilitarian finance in terms of exact policy prescriptions. As J.M. Buchanan puts it, "it becomes extremely arduous, if not impossible, to fit in the theoretical frame-work with empirical content."[11]

J.M. Buchanan has attempted to build up a theoretical case for inter-regional transference of resources through federal policy on the basis of the concept of fiscal justice. The principle of fiscal equity, as applied in the case of a federation, requires that the Central Government should take action to transfer funds from high capacity areas in order to equalize the fiscal pressure on each living in different state. The Central Finance authority must enter the process and treat equals inequality in order to offset the divergences in the income and wealth levels of the subordinate unites.

But the theoretical case for the inter-regional transference of resources based upon the concept of fiscal equity has certain limitations in practice. The concept of fiscal equity is based upon the "quid pro quo" idea of public finance and ignores the consideration of economic development and stabilization. Besides, it is difficult to ascertain the aggregate common benefits from public services to specific individuals. A substantial part of public funds is spent for the general welfare and it is difficult in such cases to determine the benefit accruing to each individual.

Fiscal policy in a federal state has to transfer resources from a line having lower marginal productivity to one having a higher one. But the transfer of government income from a high income state to low income one through federal fiscal weapon tend to retard the inceptive to labour mobility and thus prevent the maximization of national production. On the other hand, it has been maintained that such income transfers will tend to retard the movement of resources towards their most productive employments. In each case the result will depend upon the way and mode of transfer. "In most cases the transfers seem to have the effect of encouraging the flow of resources in the direction indicated by the market criteria. But the validity of the above conclusion depends primarily upon the model of low income state which is taken into consideration. According to Scott, a low income state is one where both national resources and other factors are scarce and the national product will be highest only when the scarce labour, capital and enterprise are attracted to the best soil, ports, mines, sites, etc. and that federal transfers are guided by the objective of maximizing production. On the other hand, Buchanan model of low income state is conceived in terms of scarcity of capital, abundance of unskilled labour and equal endowment of other natural resources and he thought his model to be most "representative of reality". But both Scott and Buchanan model is not comprehensive. There might be state conforming closely to the model of Buchanan and there might be numerous individual variations conforming to neither of the models. On the whole, it may be concluded that federal transfers tend to conform to the criteria of allocative efficiency and to the growth of the national output only to the extent to which such transfers result in a higher marginal productivity of resources in the low income states. But in a federal structure the criteria of allocative efficiency may not be the sole consideration in the policy of inter-regional transference of resources. The very nature of the federal structure might compel to take other factors like "equity, national interest and the preservation of minimum standard of the public services into account."

It is maintained that the plan of economic development in a developing economy must be guided by the objective of attaining regional or geographical balance in development. But the growth objective and distributive objective clash, federal government should be motivated primarily by the consideration of maximizing the rate of economic growth. Mr. K.V.S. Shastri observing on the conflicting objective of federal finance to promote economic growth and reduce interpersonal and inter-regional disparities in wealth and income, submits that in every country, operating development plans, a compromise has to be effected between the conflicting objectives of growth and distribution. From the regional point of view, the demand for a mitigation of inter-regional inequalities in per capita incomes and the ensuring of a minimum per capita income in any region is likely to derive considerable political strength, while the rate of growth of income has to be raised in the light of the availability of resources for development.

## Notes and References

1. A.H. Birch, Federalism, Finance and Social Legislation in Canada, Australia and U.S., p. 306.
2. Encyclopedia Britannica, U.S.A., 1982, 1990.
3. General Studies, Unique Publishers, New Delhi, 1989, p. 37.
4. B.D. Basu, Introduction to the Constitution of India, Prentice Hall of India Private Ltd., New Delhi, 1980, p. 280.
5. Coffee Board *Vs.* C.T.O., A.I.R. 1971 S.C.P. 870.
6. R.K. Sinha: Evolution of Fiscal Federalism in India, South Asian Publication Pvt. Ltd., New Delhi, 1981, p. 2.
7. *Ibid.*, p. 7.
8. M.V. Pylee: Constitutional Government in India, Asia Publishing House, 1977, p. 618.
9. P.K. Jha, Federal Finance in Development of India, Capital Publishing House, Delhi, 1983, p. 5.
10. *Ibid.*, p. 6.
11. *Ibid.*, p. 10.
12. *Ibid.*, p. 11.

# 2

# Union-State Fiscal Relation in India

## (I) BRIEF SURVEY OF UNION-STATE FISCAL RELATION BEFORE GOVERNMENT OF INDIA ACT, 1935

### (I)

The finances during the East India Company's regime were characterized by excessive centralization which resulted in provincial extravagance and negligence of local officers. The provincial Government resented the interference of the central authority, whose control could not be effective due to the absence of modern methods of accounting and auditing and of rapid means of communication made worse, in the earlier years, by the separation of the company's territorial areas by independent territories. During the company's regime, the condition of Indian finance was one of "chronic deficits". Since 1813, when the commercial accounts of the company were separated from its territorial revenue and expenditure and until the end of its rule in 1858, there was a surplus of £8.9 million in 13 years of surplus as against deficit in 33 years amounting to £72.2 million. The company was ceaselessly engaged in aggressive wars continuously swelled its military expenditure.

The expenditure on civil administration was high owing to the exclusion of Indians from higher appointments and it increased with the expansion of the company's territory. Till 1813, there was also the strain of expenditure on the company's investment estimated at nearly £1.2 million annually. A certain proportion of the revenue of Bengal had been for many years set apart in the purchase of goods for export to England, and this was called the investment. The company's expenditure rose from £6.9 million in 1792-93 to £41.1 million in the last year of its rule. The entire revenues were raised in India but a substantial proportion of them were spent in England—this duality of spending authority was not conductive to efficient expenditure control. No attempt was made to check the growth of expenditure except the notable decrease from £24.2 million in 1828 to £16.7 million in 1835 as a result of the efforts of Lord Bentinck.

The most important source of income was land revenue. The other sources of revenue, in order of importance, being the optimum monopoly, salt revenues, customs (the duties never exceeded 10 percent), abkari or excise and stamps. The company never cared to develop the resources of the country or to provide nation-building, social and development services, though a beginning was made in these directions.

## (2)

At the outset, the entire revenues of the country were pooled into a single central fund, from which the Government of India met its own expenditure as also that of the provincial Governments. Most of the revenue was collected by the provinces, which were also responsible for disbursing a large proportion of it. As increased revenues or economy in expenditure brought no local advantage, the system was not conductive to efficient management of finances. This extreme centralization led to constant disputes as the provinces had to obtain the approval of the Central Government even for minor items of expenditure. They were more impressed by their own needs and could not appreciate the financial difficulties of the Central Government, which was also not familiar with local problems and was unable to stop provincial extravagance. To remove these defects Lord Mayo, by his Resolution of December 14, 1870 introduced these system of making fixed grants to the provinces for meeting the cost of provincial services, and any extra expenditure on these was to be met by effecting economy or imposing local taxes. A lump sum grant of £4.7 million a year, in addition to the departmental receipts from these services, was made for the provincial services on jails, registration, police, education, medical, printing, roads, civil buildings and miscellaneous public improvements. In the central accounts, these were replaced by the single item, "provincial services". The provinces were given some freedom to appropriate this grant within the several heads and any unspent grant could be carried forward. However, as the need for a strong Central Government was paramount, a number of restrictions were continued to enable the Government of India to retain its controlling and supervisory powers.[1]

The next step forward was taken in 1877, under Lord Lytton, when all the remaining services (along with the connected receipts) except those directly administered by the Government of India, were transferred to the provinces. To meet the extra expenditure, the provinces were given a share of revenue (from excise, stamps and some other items that varied from province to province), which suffered from neglect due to absence of any provincial interest in their collection. If the actual revenue from these heads differed from the estimated realization, the provinces were to share the excess or deficit with the Government of India in equal proportion. Thus, for the first time, the provinces were given a direct interest in the collection of revenue. These contracts were different for different provinces and were subject to revision after five years. When they were revised in 1882, Lord Mayo's lump sum grants were abolished and the provinces were assigned, besides the departmental receipts, a specified share from the revenue heads already transferred to them and a fixed share of land revenue to make up the deficit in their budgets. When these quinquennial settlements were revised in 1904, and attempt was made to give the same share of the chief sources of revenue to the provinces so as to achieve equality of treatment and the revenue from excise, stamps, income tax, registration, forest, larger irrigation works and land revenue was shared generally in equal proportion between the two Governments. The share of the "divided heads" were not always the same for all provinces. For example, while the united provinces received three-eighths of land revenue, Bengal's share was one-half. This resulted in deficits or surpluses in provincial budgets which were adjusted through fixed cash assignments from the central or provincial share of land revenue to the other Government. The provinces also received the departmental receipts, registration fees and minor irrigation receipts and were responsible for expenditure on these heads. The charges on the "divided heads" were shared equally between the two Governments except that expenditure in connection with land revenue including district administration was a provincial liability.

The periodical revision of the contracts caused resentment amongst the provinces as the Government of India would try to appropriate to itself most of the improvement in provincial finances. It was not conductive to continuity of financial policy and encouraged hasty and extravagant expenditure by the provinces in the last year of the contracts. The expenditure on Home Charges, incurred in England, caused uncertainty due to a falling exchange rate since the process of decentralization began and imposed a heavy strain on central finance. By now, the central budget was no longer a gamble in foreign exchange. Accordingly, the settlements made in 1904 were declared quasi-permanent. After a few changes (such as a larger share of excise revenue to the provinces by reducing the fixed cash assignments from land revenue) the settlements made after 1911 were declared permanent. However, the Government of India was to assist a province in case of widespread famine and call for aid from the provinces in case of war or serious financial crisis.

The history of financial decentralization shows that this process evolved and progressed on considerations of administrative convenience rather than any regard to the principles of finance appropriate to a vast country having wide regional disparities. The arrangements involved gross inequalities between the provinces inter so as no regard was paid to the wealth, population, per capita income or need of the provinces in allocating funds to them. Against this must be said that the Government of India was not proceeding on a clean state and the satisfactory available basis was the actual level of expenditure attained in each province though, to achieve a semblance of equity, subsequent revisions always favoured the weaker provinces. The aim of these steps towards decentralization was to achieve economy in expenditure and efficiency in revenue collection and they were justified by these tests. The arrangements were occasionally disturbed in emergencies when the provinces were asked to make special contributions, which were remitted later. The Government of India gave special grants in surplus year and this had a distorting influence on provincial finance. It never relinquished its supremacy and throughout retained its overall control over the financial administration, including creation of posts and revision of salary scales, of the provinces. It felt that responsibility for provincial solvency must rest with itself under an administration that was not responsible to the people. For this reason, the provinces could not budget for a deficit and were not given the right to raise loans or impose fresh taxation. In their zeal for improvement of local services, they might impose heavy burdens on the people which might be resented and add to the unpopularity of foreign rule.

**(3)**

The reforms of 1919 saw the beginning of the new objective of provisional autonomy. The "divided heads" were abolished. Land revenue, excise, stamps, forests, registration and irrigation works, were wholly provincialized, while opium, salt, custom, income tax, railways, posts and telegraphs and military receipts were wholly central. The provinces were also made responsible for the expenditure on irrigation and famine. These changes left the Government of India with a deficit. The Meston Committee estimated that, as a result of the constitutional changes, the provinces had an extra spending power of Rs. 18.50 crores at the cost of the Government of India. Accordingly, it fixed the provincial contributions to cover the central deficit, estimated at Rs. 9.83 crores, as a proportion of the addition to the spending power of the different provinces. The Meston Settlement (1920) resulted in great inequalities, for example, the contribution of Tamil Nadu was Rs. 348 lacks and of the United Provinces Rs. 240 lacks, as against that of Maharashtra Rs. 56 lacks and of Bengal Rs. 63 lacks. This was strongly resented. Against the expectations of the Meston Committee, the provinces faced budgetary deficits. The contribution of Bengal had to be remitted successively from 1922-23. Further, as a result of improvement in Central Finance, the contributions were partly remitted (Rs. 2.50 crores) in 1925-26 and (a further Rs. 1.25 crores) in 1926-27. They were wholly remitted in 1927-28 and were finally abolished in 1928-29. The provinces were given powers of taxation and borrowing subject to the control of the Government of India. The provinces had the system of diarchy, whereby the provincial subjects were divided into "Reserved" and "Transferred". The "Transferred" subjects, consisting of social and nation building services, were under the charge of Minister responsible to the provincial legislatures. The provincial Governors had powers of restoring any cuts by the legislature in the "Reserved' subjects but were bound by its resolution on the "Transferred" subjects. The provincial resources were to be used in the following order: first, contribution to the Government of India; secondly, needs of the reserved subjects; and thirdly, the requirements of the transferred heads. Thus, additional taxation would seem to be necessitated by the needs of the transferred subjects. Though the Central Legislative Assembly had an elected majority possessed some control over a small proportion of the central budget, this concession was nullified by giving to the Viceroy the power of certifying the budget if it was not passed by the Assembly.[2]

## (II) FINANCIAL PROVISIONS UNDER GOVERNMENT OF INDIA ACT, 1935

Part vii of the Act of 1935 embodied the statutory provisions relating to finance. However, to grasp the implications of the financial scheme fully, it would be necessary to study it in the context of 'special responsibilities' and 'discretionary powers' of the Governor-General and the Governor. A reference to the provisions dealing with 'legislative procedure' would also be necessary.

Section 136 defined Federal revenue as "all revenues and public moneys raised or received by the Federation", and provincial revenues as "all revenues and public money raised or received by a province". The definition, as such, included not only the normal, recurrent income, but also the extraordinary non-recurrent receipts, e.g., borrowed funds or the proceeds of the sale of property.

Certain revenue were to be levied and collected by the Federal Government, and distributed among the Federating Units in accordance with the principles of distribution formulated by the Act of the Federal legislature. the Federal legislature, was entitled to increase the said duties or taxes by levying a surcharge for Federal purposes. The following sources of revenue were specified under this category:

(1) Succession duties on property other than agricultural land;
(2) Stamp duties mentioned in the Federal Legislative List;
(3) Terminal taxes on goods or passengers carried by railway or air; and
(4) Taxes on railway fares and freights.

The Federal government was to levy and collect taxes on income other than agricultural income. A prescribed percentage of the annual net proceeds of income tax, except in so far as those proceeds' represented proceeds attributable to Chief Commissioner's provinces or to taxes payable in respect of Federal emoluments, was to be assigned to the provinces and to the Federal states, if any, within which the tax was to be levied in that year. It was provided that the percentage originally prescribed could not be increased by any subsequent order in council, and that the Federal legislature was authorized to increase the said taxes at any time by levying a surcharge for Federal purposes.

Sub-sections (2) of section 138, enabled the Federation to retain, for its own purposes, a prescribed sum from the money assigned to the provinces or the Federal states under sub-section (1) of section 138. The Federation was entitled to retain:

(a) "in each year of a prescribed period such sum as may be prescribed; and
(b) In each year of a further prescribed period a sum less than that retained in the preceding year by an amount, being the same amount in each year, so calculated that the sum to be retained in the last year of the period will be equal to the amount of each annual reduction".

Section 139 deal with the 'Corporation Tax', a tax levied on the capital, or other standard indices of the companies' wealth. In view of item 46 of the Federal Legislative List (Schedule vii) the corporation Tax appeared to be meant entirely for the purpose of the Federal Government'. Owing to the insistence of the Indian rulers on their rights in respect of levying and collection of taxes at the Third Round Table Conference, the Act granted numerous exemptions to the Indian State with regard to Corporation Tax.

The proceeds of salt duties, Federal duties of excise, and export duties normally belonged to the Federation which was also the levying and collecting authority. But if an Act of the Federal Legislature so provided, the provinces 'and the states, if any', were to be paid a sum equivalent to the whole or any part of the net proceeds of the above description, and the distribution among the provinces, do, etc. was to be made in accordance with principles formulated by the Act. With regard to the exports duty on jute products it was laid down, that one half, or such greater portion as His Majesty in Council might determine, of the net proceeds in each year, was to be assigned to the provinces (or Federal State if any) in which jute was grown in proportion to the respective amounts of jute grown therein.

No bill or amendment imposing or varying any tax or duty in which 'provinces were interested', or varying the meaning of the expression 'agricultural income', or affecting the principles on which money was to be distributed to provinces or states, or imposing any Federal surcharge, could be introduced or moved in the Federal legislature without the previous sanction of the Governor-General in his discretion. Before giving his sanction to the imposition of a Federal surcharge, the Governor-General was required to satisfy himself that all practicable economies and all practicable measures for otherwise increasing the proceeds of Federal revenue were inadequate.

Assistance to deficit provinces to the extent of "such sums as may be prescribed by His Majesty in Council "chargeable on the revenue of the Federation in each year, was to be extended as grants-in-aid.

Section 143 provided that "Any taxes, duties, cesses of fees which, immediately before the commencement of Part III of this Act, were being lawfully levied by any Provincial Government, municipality or other local authority or body under a law in force on the first day of January 1935, may, notwithstanding that those taxes, duties, cesses or fees are mentioned in the Federal Legislative List, continue to be levied and to be applied to the same purposes until provisions to the country is made by the Federal Legislature".

The Governor-General and the Governor of a province were to make rules for the purpose of securing that all moneys received on account of the revenues of the Federation or of the province, were paid, withdrawn and kept in custody in a prescribed way.

Section 154 exempted Federal property from provincial taxation, and section 155 rendered provincial property immune to Federal taxes. The provinces, however, were not exempted from Federal taxation in respect of trade or business carried on by or on behalf of the Provincial Government in any part of British India outside that province.[3]

### Borrowing and Audit

During the discussions in the Federal Finance Committee, grievances were voiced by provincial representatives regarding their limited borrowing powers. The First peel committee expressed itself opposed to the exercise of complete Federal control over internal borrowings by a provinces. It, however, favoured the Federal Government, to be provided with a "suitably restricted power of control over the time at which provinces should issue loans."

The Act (1935) laid down that the executive authority of a province extended to borrowing upon the security of the revenues of the province. Subject to such conditions as it thought fit to impose, the Federation could make loans to, or, so long as any limits fixed under sub-section (1) of section 163, were not exceeded, give guarantees in respect of loans raised by any province.

Consent of the Federation was necessary to enable a province to borrow outside India or to raise any loan while any part of Federal loan made to the province or of a loan in respect of which the Federation or the Governor-General-in-Council had given a guarantee remained unpaid. All disputes relating to the justifiability of 'a refusal of consent, or a refusal to make a loan or to give a guarantee, or any condition insisted upon' by the Federation were to be referred to the Governor-General for his decision.

### Audit and Accounts

An Auditor General of India was to be appointed and his service conditions prescribed by His Majesty. He was to perform such duties and exercise such powers in relation to the accounts of the Federation and of the provinces as were prescribed by rules made under an order of His Majesty in Council or by any subsequent Act of the Federal legislature varying or extending such an order.

However, no Bill or amendment for the aforesaid purpose could be introduced or moved without the previous sanction of the Governor-General. After the expiration of two years from the commencement of Part III of the Act, and on the initiative of a provincial legislature, an Auditor General for a province could also be appointed by His Majesty.

With the approval of the Governor-General, the Auditor General of India was to prescribe the form in which the accounts of the Federation were to be kept and it was the duty of every Provincial Government to comply with the directions given by the Auditor General of India with regard to the methods or principles of maintaining provincial accounts. His reports on Federal and provincial accounts were to be submitted to the Governor-General and the Governor respectively who in their turn were to place them before the Federal or the Provincial Legislature.[4]

## Financial Power of the Governor

The Governor had far-reaching powers in financial statement of the estimated receipts and expenditure of the province, before the provincial legislature and was empowered to direct the inclusion of such sums in the financial statement as were considered necessary by him for the due discharge of any of his special responsibilities.

The estimates of expenditure embodied in the annual financial statement were to show separately 'expenditure charged on the revenues of the province' and 'other expenditures' proposed to be made from the revenues of the province Estimates of expenditure of the former category were not to be submitted to the vote of the Legislative Assembly. To this category of expenditures belonged the salary and allowances of the Governor and his office; debt charges, sinking found charges, redemption charges; salaries and allowances of ministers and the High Court Judges; expenditure on the administration of excluded areas; sums required to satisfy judgment pr award of any court or tribunal, etc. any question whether any proposed expenditure belonged to this category or not was to be decided by the Governor in his discretion.

The Provincial Legislative Assembly had power to assent or to refuse assent to estimates categorized as "other expenditure". However, no demand for a grant could be initiated, except on the recommendation of the Governor.

The grants approved by the Provincial Assembly and the sums required to meet the expenditure charged on the revenues of the Province were to be authenticated by the Governor under his signature. The Governor was also authorized to restore the reductions made by the Legislative Assembly in respect of any demands for a grant if he felt the refusal or reduction 'would affect the due discharge of any of his special responsibilities'. A schedule specifying the sums authenticated and restored by the Governor was to be laid before the Assembly but it was not open to discussion or vote.

Section 81 referred to the laying before the legislature by the Governor of a supplementary financial statement if and when further expenditure from the revenue of the province became necessary.

The Governor's recommendation was essential for the introduction of a Bill or amendment in the Provincial Assembly making provision "for imposing or increasing any tax; or for regulating the borrowing of money or the giving of any guarantee by the province; or for amending the law with respect to any financial obligations undertaken, or to be undertaken by the province; or for declaring any expenditure to be expenditure charged on the revenues of the provinces, or for increasing the amount of any such expenditure". No Bill involving expenditure from the revenues of a province could be passed unless the Governor had recommended it to the legislature.

Section 83 secured educational grants for the benefit of the Anglo-Indian and the European Communities, and responsibility of the Governor for safeguarding the legitimate interests of minorities.

A one-man Committee composed of Sir Otto Niemeyer was appointed on December 6, 1935 to inquire and review the matters referred to under section 138(1) and (2), 140(2) and 142 of the Government of India Act. On April 6th 1936 Sir Niemeyer submitted his report in the proposals of the Niemeyer Committee, after an exchange of views between the Provincial Governments, the Government of India and the Secretary of Parliament. The Government of India (Distribution of Revenues) Order, 1936 gave validity to the proposals.

### Income Tax

Niemeyer was required to make recommendations on three points in connection with income tax—

(1) The percentage of income tax to be distributed among the provinces;
(2) The duration of each of the two periods into which the initial and permanent assignment of income tax to Provinces was to be divided, and
(3) The basis of distribution of income tax among the different Provinces.

The percentage of the income tax which was to be distributed among the Provinces was fixed at 50 per cent. On the question of retention by the Federation for a specified period of a certain amount out of the 50 per cent share of the Provinces, Sir Otto recommended that "The initial prescribed period under section 138(2)(a) being five years, the prescribed sum which during that period the Centre may in any year retain out of the assigned 50 per cent, shall be the whole or such sum as is necessary to bring the proceeds of the 50 per cent share to the Centre together with any General Budget receipts from the railways upto Rs. 13 crores, whichever is less". During a second prescribed period of five years the centre was to relinquish to the Provinces by equal steps so much of the Provincial share as it was retaining in the last year of the first prescribed period of five years, so that within about ten years from the commencement of the Provincial Autonomy, the Provinces were allowed to enjoy their full share of revenue from the income tax. The following proportions were specified for distribution, among the Provinces of the amounts available in respect of the 50 per cent share of residual taxes on income:

| *Provinces* | *Percentage (%)* |
|---|---|
| Chennai (Madras) | 15 |
| Bombay | 20 |
| Bengal | 20 |
| United Provinces | 15 |
| Punjab | 8 |
| Bihar | 10 |
| Central Provinces | 5 |
| Assam | 2 |
| N.W.F.P. | 1 |
| Orissa | 2 |
| Sindh | 2 |
| **TOTAL** | **100** |

On the question of assignment of proportion of Jute duty to the Jute growing Provinces, Sir Otto recommended 62.5% per cent as the share of the jute growing Provinces.

About the Provincial debts, he recommended that all debt contracted by Bengal, Assam, Bihar, N.W.F.P. and Orissa with the Centre prior to April 1936, be cancelled. The financial relief resulting from the said cancellations was calculated as follows:

| | |
|---|---|
| Bengal | Rs. 33 Lakhs |
| Bihar | Rs. 22 Lakhs |
| Assam | Rs. 15.5 Lakhs |
| N.W.F.P. | Rs. 12 Lakhs |
| Orissa | Rs. 9.5 Lakhs |

Regarding the Central provinces, Sir Otto recommended cancellation of all deficit debts as on March 31, 1936 and of a few of the pre-reform debts, giving the Province a relief of 15 lakhs of rupees.

In view of special relief requirements of certain Provinces, the following grants-in-aid, under section 142 of the Act, were recommended:

| | | |
|---|---|---|
| United Provinces | Rs. 25 Lakhs | For a fixed period of 5 years from the commencement of provincial autonomy. |
| Assam | Rs. 30 Lakhs | -- |
| North West Frontier Province | Rs. 100 Lakhs | Subject to reconsideration at the end of 5 years. |
| Orissa | Rs. 40 Lakhs | With Rs. 7 Lakhs additional in the first year, and Rs. 3 Lakhs additional in each of the next 4 years. |
| Sindh | Rs. 105 Lakhs | For ten years, with Rs. 5 Lakhs additional in the first year; Rs. 80 Lakhs, for the next twenty years, Rs. 65 Lakhs for the next five years; Rs. 60 Lakhs for the next five years and Rs. 55 Lakhs for the next five years. |

**Review of Financial Relations**

Under the new scheme the provincial finance did enter a distinctly Federal phase, which, however "did not revolutionize the financial system but only marked an advanced stage in its evolution." Though the resources placed at the disposal of the provinces under the Act of 1935 were undoubtedly more elastic than those provided by the Mont-Ford-Reforms, it has to be noted that most of the provincial sources were in the nature of direct taxes not capable of expansion with the increasing needs of the Provinces. Land revenue, the most important 'direct tax' allocated to the Provinces, was permanently fixed in some provinces and had recorded substantial reduction owing to the prevalence of worldwide depression. Succession duties and taxes on agricultural income were least susceptible to expansion or increase.

The most important indirect tax providing the provinces their next largest chunk of revenues was excise. Enlightened public opinion was, however, intent upon pursuing a policy of prohibition and consequently excise revenue receipts of the Provincial Government were reduced between 1930 and 1934 by about Rs. 5 crores. On the other hand, the Central heads of revenue like income tax and customs were capable of immense expansion. The principle of subventions to deficit Provinces was not clearly envisaged and the two Presidency Provinces of

Bengal and Bombay received excessive benefits at the cost of other Provinces.

The Niemeyer Report tilted the scales heavily in favour of the Centre. In the form of subventions the old system of 'Doles' reappeared. 'The industrial provinces scored heavily over the agricultural provinces while the Centre remained entrenched in its power and privilege'. The source of revenue were so divided that provincial prosperity and development were subordinated to central security. A conference of Provincial Finance Ministers held in June 1937 at Bombay expressed the view 'that all elastic sources of revenue had been collared by the Government of India, that the possibilities of the Provinces' floating loans were practically non-existent.

Though no special responsibility was imposed on the Governor for the finances of the Province, Professor K.T. Shah has contended that if sections 78 and 80 were read together with section 82, it would be apparent that the Constitution Act (1935) vested in the Governor, far reaching and overriding financial powers. It may further be pointed out that sub-section (2) of Section 141 was intended to enable the Governor-General to ensure the necessary economies in the provincial expenditure.

It is apparent that though the financial provisions of the Act of 1935 were undoubtedly more generous than those of the Act of 1919, it would be unrealistic to accept them as conforming to the principle of fiscal autonomy. The power of the purse, which constitutes the very root of the authority of a popularly-elected legislature, was bestowed on the Provincial legislatures in such a stinted and truncated fashion that the dice were heavily loaded against those who sought to make Provincial Autonomy yield results. The allocation of the sources of revenue between Centre and the provinces resulted into making all provinces deficit provinces. The scheme of 1935 left untouched and unsolved the fundamental problem of Indian finance- the securing of adequate financial resources for the Provinces.[5]

## Conclusion

In the light of the above analysis of the Centre-Provincial relations under the Act of 1935, it can be surmised that the real and effective power remained secured in the hands of the Central Government.

In terms of its contents the Act of 1935 crystallized the victory of the conservative elements in British politics.

Effective suppression of the national movement under the iron hand policy of Lord Willingdon, disintegration and disillusionment pervading the nationalist camp, growing communalization of the Indian politics, and successful dovetailing of the issue of constitutional development to the problems of minorities, depressed classes and the Indian princes, coinciding with the emergence of conservative majority in the British Parliament, furnished the uncongenial political climate in which the Act was devised and passed. Weakening of the active and operative nationalist forces in India stripped the nationalist demands of much of their legitimacy and pressure; and their supporters in the parliament, already in minority, were deprived of much of the sanction behind their convictions and utterances. The conservative spokesman on the other hand, as is evident from the speeches of Winston Churchill quoted in the preceding pages, were fast gaining in eloquence and determination in propounding their 20th century version of colonialism. Conceived in the above setting, the Act of 1935 was, in effect a thoroughly conservative piece of enactment in which the democratic concepts—like Provincial Autonomy, accountability of the executive to the legislature, federalism, judicial supremacy, and elective principle-were diluted to perfection and were subordinated to their core to the caprice and discretion of their irresponsible colonial chief executives both at the centre, and in the provinces, to preserve and contain the 'brightest jewel' of the British Empire. A close hierarchical relationship between these chief executives ensured the operation of a truly centralized system of government in India.

In the context of the strong centre, however, what needs to be understood is that centralization of power and its placement in the British hands was an imperial as well as an administrative necessity. "To hold India, the British had to control it, and as a result of their tightening control the balance of power tipped heavily towards the central government." Improvement in the means of communication during the British times enabled the central government to wield its powers more effectively and resulted in the curtailment of authority and initiative of the regional governments. Apparently, the general acceptance of the 1935 scheme of division of power between the centre and the units, by the Constituent Assembly of free India and the resultant establishment of a 'cooperative federalism' can only be explained in terms of administrative necessity of a centralized authority for India in the context of its immense diversities. The only suitable governmental system for India is one in which local initiative and strong central controls are blended together.[6]

It is clear from the above analysis that the financial system embodied in the 1935 Act was drawn in the perspective of making Federal Government much stronger. For the Britishers financially prosperous Federal Government was essential for the unity and strength of India and it would have been much injurious if anything like a residual power had been granted to the provinces.[7]

## (III) FINANCIAL POWER UNDER INDIAN CONSTITUTION

In matters of financial relations our constitution provides for a financially strong centre. Following the precedent set in the Government of India Act 1935, the constitution seeks to make a more or less clear division of financial resources between the centre and the states. The constitution is quite meticulous in working out the division of functions and tax powers with the objective of achieving maximum operational efficiency

Each tax, to the extent possible, has been assigned exclusively to that layer of government: which is best placed to levy and collect it. Overlapping of tax jurisdictions has been totally avoided.

Many of the taxes allocated to the state governments are related to land and agriculture; for example, land revenue, income tax on agriculture income, succession duty and estate duty in respect of agricultural land. In addition to these, states can levy excise duties on alcoholic liquors and narcotics and taxes on professions and callings, vehicles, passengers travelling by road or inland waterways, luxuries and amusements, and subject to certain limitation, sales and purchases of goods. Presently sales tax and state excise duties are by far the most important source of 'own' revenue for the state government.

Most of the taxes relating to industrial activity and having an inter-state base have been allocated to the central government. These include taxes on non-agricultural income, corporation tax, customs duties; excise duties except those mentioned in the state list, taxes on the capital value of assets of individuals and companies; estate and succession duties on property other than agricultural land; taxes on the sale and purchase of newspapers and advertisements therein and on the sale and purchase of goods in the course of inter-state trade. The residual power of levying all taxes not mentioned in the state list and the concurrent list also rests with the central government.

### Borrowing Powers

Articles 292 and 293 of the constitution regulate the borrowing powers of the central and state governments. Under Article 292, the central government can borrow on the security of the Consolidated Fund of India within and outside the country subject to the limits specified by the borrow only within the territory of India subject to the condition that a state may not raise any loan without the consent of the centre if there is any outstanding loan from the centre to the state or an outstanding loan for which the central government has given a guarantee. By and large this qualifying provision affects all the state governments because there is no state which is not under the centre's debt. As a result, in practice, borrowings by the states come to be regulated by the central government, which acts in the matter on the advice of India and the Union Ministry of Finance.

## Resource Transfers

The distribution of revenue raising powers which has been outlined earlier leaves the states with inadequate resources for meeting their governmental responsibilities. The framers of the constitution were aware of these imbalances between the functions and the resources of the states. Accordingly, they made provisions for resource transfers from the centre to the states. These provisions bear a very close resemblance to the corresponding provisions of the Government of India Act 1935. It seems that the financial plan of the 1935 act was retained by the framers of constitution because of the difficulties of devising a new distribution and the break with continuity it would entail.

These resource transfers take place in the form of revenue sharing and grants-in-aid. The first form of revenue sharing involves certain taxes listed under Article 268, which are levied by the centre but are collected and retained by the states. Stamp duties and excise duties on medicinal preparations are included in this category.

Secondly, there are certain taxes and duties, listed under Article 269, which are levied and collected by the centre but the whole net proceeds are assigned to the states in which the taxes are levied. These taxes and duties include succession and estate duty in respect of property other than agricultural land; terminal taxes on goods or passengers carried by railway, sea or air, taxes on railway fares and freights; taxes other than stamp duties on stock exchange and future market transactions; taxes on the sale and purchase of goods, including newspapers and advertisements therein, where the transaction takes place in the course of inter-state trade and commerce.

Article 270 of the constitution requires the central government to assign to the states a part of the income tax revenue. Provision for the permissive sharing of excise revenue has been made under Article 272. Both the collective and individual shares of the states have been left undefined, to be determined by the central government in accordance with the recommendations of a Finance Commission for which provision has been made under Article 280(3) of the constitution.

Finally, there is a provision for central grants-in-aid to state governments under Articles 275 and 282. Various clauses of Article 275 provide for both general and specific grants. However, it has been left to the parliament to decide which states are in need of grant assistance and to what extent subject to the recommendations of the Finance Commission. Article 282 provides for grants from one government to another for any public purpose, whether or not this purpose is constitutionally within the jurisdiction of the donor government.[8]

From the standpoint of the constitution, the states shares of the revenue raised by the centre are fully determined by Articles 268, 269, 270 and 272 which deal with the distribution of certain taxes and duties and by Article 275 which deals with grant-in-aid to state in need of assistance. The logical inference is that Article 282 was intended, not to enable the centre to make regular grants to a state, but to serve as a residuary provision, enabling the centre as well as states to make grants for any public purpose. The original intention of Article 282 seems to have been that specific purpose grants under this Article would be made only in unusual circumstances. A close examination of the financial provisions of the constitution indicates that it is based upon the assumptions that the financial transfers from the centre to the states would usually consist of the shared tax revenues and the grants-in aid under Article on the advice of the Finance Commission. For the constitution, the Finance Commission would be the real custodian of the arrangements relating to federal fiscal relationships.

## An Appraisal

There is no denying the fact that the allocation of financial resources between the centre and the states in a federal structure is the most vital and at the same time, the most difficult problem. Hardly any federation in the world has fully solved this problem with complete success. In dealing with the problem, the framers of the constitution took the easy path of following the pattern laid down in the Government of India Act, 1935. The Government of India Act, 1935 had embodied many features of the financial system of United Kingdom with significant omissions. The framers of the constitution incorporated all such omissions which were basic to a parliamentary form of government.

The concept of parliamentary supremacy enshrined in the constitution has been borrowed from the United Kingdom. It was but natural and logical to adopt financial principles and procedures on which this supremacy largely rested.

The framers of the constitution, therefore, engrafted the United Kingdom provisions of financial control on the financial structure of the 1935 Act, made certain changes therein and adopted it as the financial section of the constitution.

The ideal of national unity, an enduring passion of the nationalist leaders during the freedom struggle era, found a safe harbor in the constitution of India. The framers made the centre the hundred eyed Argus of the constitution. They provided for an extra ordinarily strong central government, which could absorb the limited autonomous powers of states in the times of the national emergency; and assume the role of a controversial good fairy when the folly, inaptitude, ambition or extravagance of the politicians produced the breakdown of the state constitutional machinery.

Thus, the constitution makers were able to achieve their objective of a strong centre. Because there did not exist within the constituent assembly a powerful lobby of the "states' rights" men who could put up a convincing case for state autonomy, the federal scheme thus devised in the constitution, the states were given a legally inferior status. It would not be far from truth if we said that the framers of the constitution clearly intended that the state should be subordinate to the union. The supreme court in its judgment in a case between West Bengal and the Union of India expressed this intention of the founding fathers unambiguously. The majority judgment observed that "there is undoubtedly distribution of powers between the union and the states in matters legislative and executive, but distribution of powers is not always an index of political sovereignty. The exercise of powers, legislative and executive, in the allotted fields is hedged in by numerous restrictions, so that the powers of the states are not coordinate with the union and are not in many respects independent."

Taking into consideration certain fundamental features of the Constitution, such as the restrictions of the executive and legislative powers of the states and on their powers of taxation, the judgment concluded that "it would not be correct to maintain that absolute sovereignty remains vested in the states. This is illustrated by certain striking features of our constitutional set-up. There is no dual citizenship in India; all citizens are citizens of India and not of the various states in which they are domiciled. There are no independent constitutions of the states, apart from the national constitution of the union of India."[9]

This constitution thus centralizes power in the hands of the central government and it also empowers to override the states both in normal times and in times of emergency. In normal times the centre is the policeman watching the deviant states; in times of emergency it becomes the shooting soldier. In normal times, the executive powers of the states are coextensive with their legislative power; but the width of the states' executive power is severely narrowed by the provisions of the constitution dealing with the administrative relations between the centre and the states. First, the states should exercise their executive power in such a manner as to secure compliance with the laws enacted by parliament. Secondly, the states, while exercising their executive power, should not act in any way prejudicial to the exercise of the union's executive power. Lastly, the most offensive clause that pinpoints the inferior status of the states is that the union is empowered to issue necessary directions to the states to secure the two objectives. In case the states fail to comply the constitution authorizes the union to supersede the governments of the states concerned, for such non-compliance is deemed to be the breakdown of the state constitutional machinery and attracts President's rule.

During the period of national emergency the constitution ceases to be quasi-federal for the distribution of powers between the centre and the states. The centre withdraws all powers from the states and the financial support it gives them as per the recommendations of the Finance Commission. During the emergency parliament is empowered to make laws for the whole or any part of India with respect to any matters enumerated in the State List.

The constitutional provisions establish that the union government has supervisory power over the legislative and executive authority of the state. However, it is not an omnibus authority which reduces the states to that of administrative units of a unitary government as in the pre-independence period. Yet the frequency with which all manner of questions relating to administration of law and order, labour relations, etc. are raised in parliament reveals its anxiety to establish the position that it is in overall charge of India's administration, free to invade at will the legislative and executive domain of the States.

## (IV) FISCAL FEDERALISM IN USA, CANADA, AUSTRALIA AND DEVELOPING NATIONS

The federation in U.S.A. is not only the oldest, but is also a classic model. There was no dictionary definition of federal government available for application, nor any working model for limitation, at the time when the U.S. federation was formed in 1787. The federal system devised by the founding fathers of the American Constitution as the product of necessity rather than of any doctrine. The definition of federalism which was coined later was devised on the U.S. model. The United States is now a federation of fifty sovereign States.[10]

### Separation in U.S.A.

In the United States the basic position about the distribution of financial powers has been laid down in section 8, 9 and 10 of Article 1 of the Constitution. Section 8 of the Constitution lays down that the Congress shall have powers to levy and collect taxes, duties imports and excise, to pay the debts and provide for the common defense and general welfare of the United States, but all duties, imports and excise shall be uniform throughout the country. The federal government has exclusive jurisdiction over customs while in other fields of taxation it has concurrent powers with the States. In order to avoid double taxation of the same courses, there has been devised a built-in-mechanism of tax credits which also helps in making assessments. Before the First World War, federal government had some difficulty in entering the income tax field, but the sixteenth amendment 1913, paved the way of federation to enter this field too.

The main sources of federal revenue now are both personal and corporate as Income tax; duties of excise on gasoline, tobacco and liquor taxes and death duties. The federal assessment allows tax credit for the state tax in computing the federal tax liabilities. Many States also impose corporate income tax, gasoline, tobacco and liquor taxes, as also death duties. This causes a lot of duplication and overlapping of tax jurisdiction both horizontal and vertical creating economic inefficiencies and inequities among the tax payers. Despite these imperfections, taxes on income constitute two-third of the total federal revenues. The revenue sources of the States include property tax on land, buildings and equipments, inheritance tax, income taxes, business taxes, sales tax and gasoline tax. Share of direct taxes are as large as 93 per cent in case of income taxes and 78 per cent in case of death and gift taxes. Besides, the federal government shares the indirect taxation also, its share ranging from 40 to 80 per cent.

With the emergence of depression in thirties the federal government intervened on a large scale through emergency crash programs of public works relief and welfare. Old age insurance and federal state unemployment insurance schemes were thus launched in 1935 under the Social Security Act. This raised the problem of inter-governmental transfer payments. In 1948 the federal payments to the state aggregated $1.771 million, by 1966, these payments swelled to $ 13.115 million.

## Tax-sharing in U.S.A.

It is not a common practice in U.S.A. to divide revenue from tax head between the federal and the States Governments. Suggestions have been made by the National Tax Association for Federal collection and sharing of taxes on gasoline, liquor, cigarettes and manufactures, excise, corporate and personal income-tax and inheritance tax. Tax sharing is also proposed as means to reduce federal aid. The federal credit provision is a kind of shared tax under which the federal government determines how large the tax shall be and forms part of the revenue over to the States.

## Grants-in-Aid in U.S.A

In U.S.A., the constitution does not incorporate provisions relating to grants-in-aid. The matter is left to the federal government to decide and so far it has granted assistance to the States under "welfare clause". These are entirely specific grants in which matching is insisted upon. The federal governments have shown little interest in either fiscal head grants or compensation grants. The federal grant system in United States has developed on the basis of federal grant for schools in 1785. Representative Morril of Vermont in 1862, the Morril Act, 1890, Social Security Act of 1935 and the Public Law 377 of 1946, are some of its instances.

The grant-in-aid is one of the important media of the transfer of resources from federal government to States which constituted 93 per cent of the total transfers in 1963. By 1966 this percentage rose to 95. While the close grants are determined by the Congress, the open end are based on data formulated by the Stares.

The federal grants pertaining to public assistance and highway construction are by far the most significant. The former are intended to help states implement general welfare programs and maintain them at a minimum national standard. Of these programs the two providing for old age assistance and aid to the families of dependent children and aid to the blind and disabled are significant. Through the grant-in-aid device, the federal government sets a standard of the welfare program to be followed by the States, in order to qualify for the grant.

The Public Assistances Grants constitute almost one third of the total federal grants and the highway construction grants constitute another one-third. The federal grants have redistributive effect although that was never intended by the federal authorities. The proliferation of federal grants in recent past, had however, and raised certain problems. The grants have caused the state government to change their financial decisions. The bait of federal money led the state legislatures to spend more on project of federal choice. A close analysis reveals that matching requirements of these grants absorbed larger portions of State tax revenue in poorer stares than in the rich ones. According to a study of the Advisory Commission on Inter-Governmental Relations, while the States of Delaware, Connecticut and New Jersey bore 6 per cent of their tax revenue as matching grants, the portions of less affluent states like Mississippi Sout Carollina, Arkaneas, Alabama and Tennessee ranged from 11 to 18 per cent. Further in order to manage finances for services eligible for federal aid the States would sometimes divert the state money from the services not eligible for federal aid. The Congressional Commission on inter-governmental financial relations, 1955 held that in the context of the constitutional development of United States, conditional grants represent a basically sound technique despite their piecemeal development and hotch potch appearance. The commission emphasized that grant should be made only for clearly indicated and important financial objectives, that they should be given for broad purposes like public health or welfare rather than for highly specialized schemes, that allocation should be flexible in relation to specific schemes or activities covered by these broad purposes and that matching requirements should take into account the economic conditions in the units and their fiscal capacity.[11]

## Federal Finance in Canada

British North America, as Canada was then known comprised seven British colonial provinces prior to their federation. The British North America Act, 1867, the Constitution of Canada enacted by the British Parliament paved the way for a federation. The four out of seven colonies, like other federations were an outcome of compromises. The four colonies that formed the federation in 1876 were Upper and Lower Canada, Nova Scotia and New Burnswick. The two Canadas that were formerly parts of the provinces of Canada were formally separated by the B.N.A. Act and named Ontario and Quebec respectively. The remaining colonies joined later, the last being Newfoundland which was admitted to the federation as late as 1949. At present, Canada is composed of 10 provinces and two territories. The provinces and territories and the years of their joining the federation or their creation are as follows:

| *Serial Number* | *Provinces* | *Year of joining the Federation* |
|---|---|---|
| 1. | New Foundland | 1949 |
| 2. | Nova Scotia | 1867 |
| 3. | Prince Edward Island | 1873 |
| 4. | New Brunswick | 1867 |
| 5. | Ontario | 1867 |
| 6. | Québec | 1867 |
| 7. | Manitoba | 1870 |
| 8. | Saskatchewan | 1905 |
| 9. | Alberta | 1905 |
| 10. | British Columbia | 1970 |
| **Territory** | | |
| 1. | Yukon Territory | 1898 |
| 2. | North West Territory | 1870 |

## Separation in Canada

In Canada, the confederating status conferred wide and unfettered powers of taxation to the Dominion while the taxing powers of the provinces were restricted to direct taxes in order to raise revenue for provincial purposes. These taxes in aggregate produced only one-fifth of the total revenue of the provinces in 1866. The main sources of Dominion tax revenue are taxes on personal and corporate incomes, succession and estate duties, customs and import duties, excise duties and excise taxes. The main provincial sources of tax revenue are income tax, motor vehicles, licenses and permits, succession duties, hospital insurance premiums, assessment tax, corporation tax, gasoline and general sales tax. The present financial arrangements in Canada have been influenced by the Royal Commission on Dominion provincial relations, the tax Rental Agreements in 1942 as modified in 1957, etc.

Although the circumstances prevailing in both the federations at the time of inception were widely different there is a lot of similarity in the arrangement that ultimately emerged. Both favoured a financially strong centre and, therefore, conferred taxing power in customs, excise, income and corporation taxes, and estate duties to the federal government, sales tax motor vehicles tax, and entertainment tax were allocated to the unit governments in both the countries. However, unlike Canada, tax on personal income cannot be levied by States in India except tax on professions, trades and calling which has a remote resemblance with the provincial income tax of Canada. In any case, the Canadian Dominion Government enjoys greater or more unfettered powers of taxation as compared to those enjoyed by the Union Government in India.

## Tax-Sharing in Canada

In Canada, the tax sharing arrangement, excepting in the case of income tax on power utilities has never appeared in the inter-governmental fiscal relations. "An extensive use of tax credit arrangement between the Dominion and provincial governments has been extensively used".

## Grants-in-Aid in Canada

Ever since the inception of the confederation, Canada has followed a system of unconditional federal grants to the provinces. In earlier years these grants were given largely on political rather than economic considerations. Obviously this device of assistance infringed the widely known principle of "independence and responsibility", i.e., the responsibility of raising revenue and the freedom of spending it ought to go hand to hand. The Rowell Sirpis Commission was bitter against the chaotic and illogical system of subsidies under which under grants were paid on a variety of bases and suggested their substitution by a system of two forms of grants. First, fiscal need or as the Commission called them national to enable the province to provide services at a national standard which it recommended as irreducible and secondly, emergency grants to be made only in the event of financial stringency. The Commission suggested a Permanent Finance Commission to advice upon matters of these grants every five years. During the fiscal year 1968, the Dominion Government of Canada made payments to the various provinces to the tune of $2482 million of which $1,617 million were conditional and $865 million unconditional grants which respectively constituted 15 per cent and 8 per cent of the total Dominion expenditure for that year.

In Canada, the pattern of financial relations between the dominion and the provinces has been the subject of criticism and frequent adjustments in recent years. Until the First World War, the Dominion Government had restricted itself to levying only custom and excise, leaving direct taxation to the provinces. It, however, introduced income-taxes along with sales and long range of commodity taxes during the war. Besides, sweeping economic and social changes took place in Canada since 1867 which caused the provinces to place before the Dominion authorities a demand for greater assistance to cope with the new situation. The Dominion government in response to these provincial demands introduced a system of conditional grants-in-aid for housing, highways, education and other civil needs. Again, the depression of 1930s badly shattered the foundations of the federal system and changed the whole fabric of Dominion-Provincial relations. In 1937, the Prime Minister of Canada submitted a report to the Privy Council asking for the "re-examination of the economic and financial basis of the confederation" and the appointment of a high-powered Commission under the Chairmanship of Newton Wesley Rowell to undertake the task of this re-examination.

The Royal Commission on Dominion-Provincial Relations made an extensive enquiry and submitted its report in 1940, covering almost all aspects of the inter-governmental relations. With respect to tax allocation, the Commission suggested that the personal income tax, corporation tax and death duty be permanently transferred to the Dominion government. In return, the Dominion government was asked to undertake full responsibility of employable unemployed and assume the whole provincial debt. The recommendations of the Commission were, however, never implemented. Rather the Principles underlined by it were rejected.

In the meantime, the Second World War broke out. In April 1941, the Dominion Government obtained relinquishment of the domain of income-tax—both personal and corporate—by the Provinces for the duration of war and one year after and offered compensation roughly equivalent to their collections in 1940. Thus, the provinces entered what is known as the War Time Tax Agreements, giving the Dominion a free hand in the field of income taxation. The Dominion government also established a National Unemployment Insurance Scheme and a Nation Employment Service. The termination of the war was yet another turning point in the federal financial history of Canada. Having fought the depression and the war, the Dominion government under its post-war reconstruction program undertook full cost of old age pension and unemployment assistance and extended assistance to then provinces in health insurance scheme at the rate of not less than $12 per capita. In return, the Provinces were asked to surrender to the Dominion, exclusive right to levy income taxes and death duties temporarily for five years. But the proposal did not find favour with the provinces and after negotiations for nine months under a new arrangement; Tax Rental Agreements were signed by all the provinces except Ontario and Quebec. Under this arrangement for five years, the Dominion was given sole occupancy of the domain of income taxes and succession duties. However, 5 per cent of the net corporation tax was to be turned over to the Provinces after collection by the Dominion. The agreements were renewed in 1952 and 1957 for further periods of five years with favourable terms to Provinces.

However, the provinces found them illusory and asked for better terms when time came for their renewal in 1951. Finally legislation was passed, which was to be effective from 1962, under which the tax rentals were discontinued and provinces were allowed concurrent jurisdiction over the three taxes. Federal Tax rates were also changed in order to accommodate provinces in their levies. The new arrangement was also revisable after five years.

A few changes have recently been made in the latest dominion-provincial fiscal arrangement in regard to the method of calculating the payments to be made to the provinces. Under the new scheme, any province in which average provincial tax rates would yield less revenue per capita than that in Canada as a whole would be entitled to an equalization payment. Thus, the payment will be based on differences in fiscal capacity of a province rather than on the inter-provincial differences in the cost of and need for public service, i.e. the "fiscal needs" of the provinces. In short, they will be in the nature of "revenue equalization grants".

It is interesting to note that the problems of fiscal adjustment in Canada are akin to those in India. Like Tamil Nadu in India, the province of Quebec in Canada has been fighting for financial autonomy of the states. Like the Rajamannar Committee on Centre-State relations appointed by Tamil Nadu, Quebec had appointed the Tramblay Commission in 1953 which also asked for more liberty and security for Quebec. It submitted its report in 1956. The tramblay report charged the other provinces as less faithful to federalism and willing to become colonies of the Ottawa Government.[12]

## Federal Finance in Australia

Australia is comparatively a newer federation. The federation came into existance on January 1, 1901, under the Commonwealth of Australian Constitution Act, 1900. Australia is composed of six States – New South-Wales, Victoria, Queensland, South Australia, Western Australia and Tasmania. Tasmania and Western Australia are poor states whereas New South Wales and Victoria are rich states. The remaining two states of Queensland and South Australia came in between. Both Australia and Canada are federations of Units that are widely divergent. But Australia has no such problem province as Quebee in Canada. Australia's population is half of that of Canada, the density in both being equal—five per square mile against 55 in the United States and 415 in India. The federal financial relationship in Australia is based not on any well-worked-out provisions for a perfect balance between the Commonwealth and the States. The main financial provisions of the Constitution are contained in the sections 51, 86, 87, 89, 90, 9e, 96 and 105A.

## Separation in Australia

In Australia, the Constitution has made some separation of revenue between the Commonwealth and the States. The main financial provisions of the Constitution may be summarised as follows:

(a) The Commonwealth has exclusive power to impose customs and excise duties (Sec. 86).

(b) Each of the States has full power of taxation in all other fields.

(c) Three-fourths of the revenue from customs and excise were to be turned over to the Sates during the first ten years of federation and thereafter until the parliament otherwise provided (Sec. 87).

(d) In addition for a period until the imposition of uniform duties of customs (as required by Section 88) and, thereafter, until the Parliament otherwise provided, all surplus revenue of the Commonwealth collected by it from each State was to be made over to the States by what is popularly known as "book-keeping systems" (Section 89).

(e) Commonwealth Parliament was empowered to grant financial assistance to the States during the first 10 years and thereafter until Parliament otherwise provided (Sec. 96).

(f) Commonwealth might take over the public debt of the States under agreement with them (Sec. 105A).

(g) By special agreement, Western Australia (which was disinclined to join the federation) was allowed for a period of five years on a yearly diminishing scale, to retain its customs revenue (Sec. 95).

Provisions of Sections 87, 89 and 95 have since lapsed, either because of the fulfilment of the condition imposed therein or because of the expiry of their effective periods. However, contrary to expectations, section 96 acquired a permanent character under the clause—"Until the Parliament otherwise provided. Today it has become a major and flexible instrument for enlarging Commonwealth power".

Thus, under the Constitution of Australia, the Commonwealth has exclusive power of taxation only with respect to customs and excise. In other field of taxation, the Commonwealth's power is concurrent with the States power. But the Commonwealth has no power to give priority to its right to tax over the States, right to tax so as to invade the realm of state authority. However, by judicial interpretation of section 96, the Commonwealth has been validly held empowered to exclude the States from the domain of income taxation. According to the High Court's interpretation of Section 96 of the Constitution, the Commonwealth has power to raise money in order to pay it over to or for the States, and it will be deemed to be a commonwealth purpose. Thus in Australia the authority of the Commonwealth is ultimately established.

The main sources of state taxation are the probate and succession duties, other stamp duties, the land tax, lotteries, the taxation of racing, motor vehicles, liquor and license, etc.

## Tax-Sharing in Australia

In Australia under the Bradden clause three-fourths of the customs and excise revenues were to be paid to the states during the first 10 years and thereafter as determined by an Act of Parliament. After 1910, the per capita grants were substituted for tax sharing. In 1927, this system of per capita payment was terminated under the financial agreement between the Commonwealth and the States and was substituted by fixed payments. The agreement also provided for the taking over the States, public debt by the Commonwealth and accepting responsibility for paying interest over them. It also gave statutory standing to the loan council. By this agreement, avoidable competition between the Commonwealth and the States in London money market for loans was eliminated.

However, soon it was realized that the new arrangements could not serve as a permanent solution of the federal financial problem. Some additional mechanisms were needed to bring about balance between the States. In 1931, therefore, a Commonwealth Grants Commission was established to look into the claims of the States for Commonwealth grants and after making due enquiry to furnish each year to Parliament, a report thereon, along with its recommendations.

The Commonwealth Grants Commission has, in the main, been considering the claims for special grants applied by the States. In the beginning, there were three claimant States viz., South Australia, Western Australia and Tasmania. As from 1969-70, Tasmania remains the lone claimant to get these special grants, South Australia having withdrawn from the scheme of Special grants since 1959-60 and Western Australia from 1968-69.

The Commonwealth Grants Commission bases its recommendations on the principle of financial need so as to enable the Claimant State to provide services of a similar standard as in other States, provided it makes a comparable revenue raising effort. Thus the redistribution of Commonwealth revenue among the States is a cardinal element of the Australian federal finance. The Commonwealth revenue is obtained in the form of taxes, from the people of the Commonwealth and then distributed among the State in the form of grants in lieu of taxes surrendered by them to the Commonwealth. The sums collected from a State and those allocated to it by way of Commonwealth grants producer distributive effects. In fact, as the taxation is collected in greater degree from the wealthier sections of Australia and distributed mainly on the basis of, population, the redistribution is favourable to the less fortunate States.

### Grants-in-Aid in Australia

In Australia, the Constitution does not provide for any specific grants like those found in Canada. But section 96 of the Constitution empowered the Commonwealth Parliament to grant financial assistance to the States during the first ten years and thereafter until parliament otherwise provided. Unlike Canada, the commonwealth government, with the exception of debt grants, in free to increase or reduce or even abolish grants. The Commonwealth grants are generally meant for social security, old age pension, unemployment benefit, rehabilitation of disabled, education, national highways and housing, agriculture and public health, etc. the Commonwealth Grants Commission, established in 1933, determines the special grants. In 1923, the Australian loan council was created to determine all borrowing, conversions, renewal policy, etc. The national works council established in 1943 determines the relative urgency of the loans.

In addition to the special grants, the general financial assistance grants and specific purpose grants are given by the Commission to the states.

The financial assistance grants provide about one-half of State's total budgetary revenues and are determined yearly on the basis of a formula under which the grants paid to a State in the previous year are increased in proportion to the increase in its population and in level of average wages for Australia as a whole. In addition, the betterment factor also increases the grants by further 1.2 per cent. This formula virtually results, in the long-run, in the grants growing faster than the economy as a whole. The distribution of these grants among the States *inter se*, is made in such a way that the richer States get a smaller amount per capita than the financially weaker states.[13]

## Federal Finance in Underdeveloped Countries

The experience of the older federation is not very useful in new federations because circumstances are so different. A country like Nigeria for instance is at an earlier stage of economic development than the older federations were at the time of their inception. The concept of the functions of the government in Nigeria today is much wider than it was in the United States in 1787, Canada in 1867 or Australia in 1900 and is in some respect wider than in these countries today. Moreover they vary widely. This gives rise to many problems in new federations.

In the first place the earlier federations resulted from the coming together of hither to independent units. This is no longer the case now. This difference has both political and economic implications. Secondly, although earlier federations were often extremely sensitive to economic motives, their governments were concerned with economic development and planning indirectly. There was very little control exercised over physical and economic environment as well as a lack of economic analysis of the problem of economy as a whole. In the new federations there is an attempt at overall planning. Thirdly, there is the further complication introduced by the rapid political, social and economic changes taking place in new federations. In the older federations, many years, even decades were available for adjustment to new circumstances. In the new federations, adjustments have to be made over a course of hardly more than five years in many cases. Thus, the strains on the working of the federal constitutions are different in nature and more intense in character than they were in the 19th century. This makes the lessons of older federations sometimes of doubtful relevance and sometimes actually misleading. Fourthly, federal constitutions are adjusted in preference to unitary constitutions because of the divergence between the social, ethical religious or cultural differences or between the economic interests of people who would in other respects like to share their political life. If the divergences are strongly localized as in Canada, federalism may offer a solution but where the divergences are not strongly localized, federalism may not solve the problem. Further the difference between the federation by aggregation and federation by disaggregation as in the case of India becomes important. In the case of federation by disaggregation there exists a pre-history of united administrative and fiscal systems which may make the federal constitution more biased towards the centre. Both centripetal and centrifugal forces are continuously present in a federation. The most important of these are concerned with the economic hopes of the units, either that closer integration will bring them advantages not otherwise available or that greater freedom will enable the unit to enjoy more rapid development. Fifthly, for a federal constitution to be a success, in the sense of promoting the development of democratic and responsible government together with a steady economic growth be better than a unitary government, it is necessary that the division of political and fiscal powers should each correspond with the initially desired political and economic degree of integration and sufficient flexibility should be available under the constitution to allow of easy adjustment to keep the respective powers appropriate. Re-adjustment in federal state relations may be required either because the initial requirements for successful working have not been correctly interpreted or because with the progress of development the appropriate conditions change. Sixthly, in the new federations the pace of political development is rapid. The standard of general education or even elementary literacy is much lower than it was in 19$^{th}$ century federations and the practice of democratic institutions is much less developed. A democratic understanding between the states and federal government is lacking. Administrative experience and the efficiency of the civilian in relation to the complicate work of the present day are lower than in the older federations. With limited efficient civil servant, they may be more attracted by the federal civil service where the pay is higher and the work more interesting. The result may be that the state administration suffers most in this respect. Seventhly, the new federations have to face cultural, religious and linguistic difference. Finally, the amalgamation motive on the economic side is also different from the older federations. Because of the enlarged field of public activity, the federal government will have to take a much more active part in respect of social services especially education and health and public activities including transport. In the economic sphere there is to be a large economic central sector. Fiscal Policy for the control of inflationary pressure generated by the development process will have to be largely a federal responsibility. Thus, political and social factors tend against a greater degree of integration and on the other hand, economic motives seem to tend strongly in the opposite direction. There should be desire to build a new nation and the acceptance of a national economic policy such as a maximization of a steady rate of economic growth for the federation as a whole. Besides, to ensure federal control of international stability a national fiscal policy should be operated by the federal government. But for full internal control, especially the control of inflationary pressure—inevitable in a development process, further internal fiscal instruments are essential. The very instruments are those that impinge directly on spending, saving and investing the factors that determine the size and growth of the national product. Control over these would apply that the federal government must have control over taxes on company profits and the rates and progression of personal income tax and customs duties. It is sometimes argued, that with such a control over the productive and elastic tax sources, the state cannot preserve financial autonomy. If by autonomy is meant that the states should not be dependent on the federal government for any grants, the contention that the states have to such autonomy may be true. In view of the pressure of rapid economic development and the need of a national economic development and the need of a national economic policy, interference in the financial autonomy of the States becomes necessary, Grants-in-aid of an unconditional type need not take away the fiscal autonomy. It is also to be realized that there will always be an imbalance between the revenue and expenditure of the State Governments and it is by federal grants and tax sharing that this imbalance is corrected. A federal government will also have to give differential aid to the poorer States if it is to fulfil the mandate of promoting well-balanced development. In order to be successful along these lines, federal States financial relations should be subject to periodic review. Thus so long as the federal constitution has itself left room for growth and has not shut the door on adjustments, there should not be too much trouble in keeping federal state relations in lines with current defacto relations between the opposing forces of amalgamation and separation."

In view of special problems of new federations, A.H. Birch emphasizes two general principles in the financial arrangement of all these federations. The first principle is the political one that wherever possible the responsibilities for raising and spending money should rest with the same authority. If this is the case each government can choose freely how far, if at all, it wishes to improve the standard of its services by raising the level of taxation. The voters can make their wishes felt on this matter and can also record their disapproval at the polls if they feel that their taxes have been misused. But in a federation it is rarely possible to obtain complete financial independence for each government. However when transfer payments are needed the principle of financial responsibility suggests a rule that may be generally applicable. This rule is that the federal grants should accompany conditions. The experiences in U.S.A., Canada and Australia have demonstrated that the principles of financial independence are no longer applicable in a federal structure in its strict form.

Another relevant general principle is that Government should have the fiscal powers necessary to promote economic development and maintain economic stability. This principle implies that the federal government should control the main sources of revenue as the federal government is in a better position to plan development and maintain stability. This argument only holds good if the federal government is politically stable and capable of pursuing a consistent policy. If the federal government is an uneasy coalition of groups with differing ideas about economic matters, while regional governments are stable and ambitious, the latter may be in a better position than the former to carry through scheme of economic development. This was the position in Nigeria in the years immediately before independence. In some cases the regional government may also be as well capable as the federal government in maintaining economic stability. Thus, we find that these principles though valid are not universally applicable. Federalism is based on compromise and the constitutions of the new federations mostly contain provisions which recognize the need for financial adjustments. Moreover, the rapid rate of economic development that is hoped for may make some of the financial clauses obsolete within a decade or two.

## (V) FINANCIAL AGREEMENTS IN DEVELOPING COUNTRIES

The patterns of inter-governmental financial relations in the new federations vary a good deal and for a variety of political, social and economic reasons. Thus Nigeria is now less centralized in its government than Rhodesia and Nyasaland because social diversities in Nigeria coincide approximately with regional boundaries whereas in Rhodesia and Nyasaland they do not. Indeed Rhodesia and Nyasaland and Malaysia must be put in a category apart from the other three federations. According to F.G. Karnell, the main political disputes in these federations are basically non-federal in character. In these circumstances, a centralized financial system can be agreed upon in an unstable political situation as in Rhodesia and Nyasaland. The other three federations are simpler to classify. India is the most unified in spite of territorial, religious and cultural diversities. Its economy is national one and is to some extent centrally planned. Communications between the

States are reasonably good and its government is in the hands of a strong and nationally organize political party. In Nigeria, the people of the three regions are divided by rivalries and the north is also set apart from the east and west by religious and cultural differences. The economic planning is mostly at the regional level. The West Indian federation is the most unified in the lot largely for geographical reasons. The financial arrangements in all these federations reflect also the degree of social and political unity existing there.[14]

### (a) Customs and Excise Duties

For facilitating the rate of economic growth, it is necessary that there is internal free trade and common tariff on imported goods in a federation. It follows that there is a very strong case for federal control of both import and excise duties. In most circumstances, the case for federal control of export duties is equally strong. But in Nigeria a case has been established for the regionalization of the more important export duties. In Malaysia all these duties remain in the hands of the federal government. In Rhodesia and Nyasaland the federation has powers to levy these duties on all goods except petrol which the territories are entitled to tax. However, 38 per cent of the net proceeds of export duties have to be distributed to the territories in proportion fixed by the Constitution in accordance with the recommendation of the Raisman Commission. In India these duties are federal. In Nigeria constitutional responsibility for customs and excise duties as rests with the federal government, except that the federal government refrains from levying export duties on the main items of produce including semi-processed commodities and these duties are replaced by regional states tax. It is also agreed that the regional governments will have power to tax sales of motor fuels and to fix a maximum level for import duties on motor fuel. In West Indies, import duties on cigarettes, beer spirits and petrol are levied and retained by the federal government and all other duties to be levied and retained by the units.

### (b) Income Tax

The case for federal control of company taxes is strong for two reasons; one is that overseas firms investing in underdeveloped countries normally feel more secure if their taxation is in the hands of one central government. Another aspect of this is that it is generally in the interest of the federation as a whole, if regional governments are deprived of the temptation to compete for overseas investment by lowering company taxes, or alternatively to exploit overseas companies who have made a major investment in their territories. The second season is the administrative one that regional control of company taxes leads to difficulties of assessments in the case of nationalized companies.

Similarly, federal control of personal income tax is advocated on the ground that the chances of maintaining economic stability are higher if the federal government has this weapon. Secondly those in poor countries, where there are relatively few wealthier people, the taxes on these people should accrue to the benefit of the country as a whole and not just to the region in which they live. The general argument against federal control is that this may make it impossible for the regions to attain a substantial measure of the independence. The balance of these argument vary from country to country and depend partly on other factors, such as the relative stability and degree of administrative competence of the federal and regional governments.

In Malaysia, all income taxes are federal. In Rhodesia and Nyasaland, income taxes are levied by the federation but 38 per cent of the proceeds have to be shared among the territories in proportions fixed by the Constitution. In addition, the territories may levy a surcharge of upto one-fifth of the federal tax, the surcharge being collected by the federal tax authorities on behalf of the territories. In India, company taxes are levied and retained by the federation, while personal income taxes are levied by the federation and the proceeds shared between federal and state government on the recommendations of the Finance Commissions. In Nigeria company taxes have always been and continue to be in the federal hands. But the regional governments now have sole power to levy personal income tax. It should be noted that the Constitution gives the federal government power to enter the income tax field in time of war or defense emergency but that this power will lapse when the emergency is over. In the West Indies there is concurrent jurisdiction over the taxation of income and profits subject to the provision that the federal government must not enter the field during the first five years of federation.

### (c) Federal Grants to States

In all these federations except the West Indies there is provision for federal grants to State and in all of them it is accepted that the relative needs of the States should play a part in determining the size of at least some of the grants. The main point of differences is as to whether the grants which have account of need should be clearly distinguished from the basic grants paid to correct the imbalance of revenues and expenditure. In the less unified federations there is pressure to distinguish the grants based on need from the basic grants while in the more unified federations, this is not thought necessary. Thus in Malaysia and Rhodesia and Nysaland there appear to have been no pressure to make this distinction and the basic grants are distributed among the States according to formula which take account of need. In Malaysia the

States get nearly half their total income in the form of federal capitation grants which are weighed in favour of the less populous states, while in Rhodesia and Nyasaland the largest claim of revenue in the territories is their share of federal income tax receipts which Southern Rhodesia gets 14%, Northern Rhodesia gets 18% and Nyasaland gets 6%. In both India and Nigeria controversy has risen about the desirability of separating basic grants from need grants and in each country the wealthier States have tended to favour separation more strongly than the poorer States. In India a large number of special grants are paid in respect of various disabilities and though these are subject to dispute on points of detail the principles seems to be generally accepted.

### (d) The Government Borrowing

In case of some of the older federations such as Canada and of the newer such as Rhodesia and Nyasaland, a desire to establish one large creditworthy government instead of a number of separate units which had difficulty in attracting loans, has been one of the strong motives for federation. The main problem in the field of government borrowing in a federation is to achieve some co-ordination of the borrowing by the different governments for two reasons. First, coordination avoids competition on the loan market as a result of which more favourable terms can be obtained. Secondly, by restraining irresponsible State borrowing, the federal government may be saved from the burden of having to rescue States in difficulty. The Australian solution in which both the federal and the States Governments give up their independent borrowing power to submit to the control of loan council despite its apparent success, has been followed closely only in the federation of Rhodesia and Nyasaland. In most of the new federations the field of external borrowing is simply left exclusively in the hands of the federal government. This being the case in India, Malaysia and Nigeria, the independence of the State power to borrow is severely limited. In Pakistan, the province possessed the power to borrow externally but this was subject to restriction by the federal government. An interesting arrangement was the provision for special tribunals to which States had recourse if federal refusal of provincial applications for external loans were not reasonable. Only the West Indies, where the power to borrow is on the concurrent list, has the pattern of classical federation been followed by giving the territories a measure of independence in raising external loans.

As far as internal loans are concerned in most of the federations, which the exception of Malaysia the States possess more independence in their borrowing power. In Nigeria, a measure of coordination is achieved through the Loans Advisory Board and in Pakistan the National

Finance Commission included federal and provisional borrowing within its powers of recommendations. In all six of the new Commonwealth federations, federal dominance of public borrowing is enhanced by the constitutional power given to the federal government to make loans to the States.

## (e) Emergency Provisions

In most of the new federations the need for flexibility in the face of emergencies is also provided for. The three Asian federations, India, Pakistan and Malaysia had in their Constitutions provisions that in the case of an emergency the internal or external security of the federation or its economic life, the central government should have overriding powers during emergency, including finance which would in effect temporarily convert the federation into unitary states but which would cease when the emergency ended. In Nigeria the emergency power is almost as sweeping. In the federation of Rhodesia and Nyasaland the federal government in the time of emergency is free from its obligation to share the income and profits tax and may raise external loans without the approval of Loan Council. In the West Indies, there are no specific financial emergency provisions but the federal government is entitled during the emergency to make law on territorial matters.

## (f) Inter-Governmental Financial Institutions

The role of Inter-governmental financial institutions in a federal system of finance is of great value and nearly all the new federations have created this institution almost on Australia model. These institutions serve two broad purposes. First, they enable co-operation in finance and in economic planning between federal and state government. Secondly, these institutions make possible a regular process of adjustment in finances and economic planning between federal and state government to meet new conditions. The problems with which these financial institutions can deal can be listed under six general headings, viz.. tax distribution, grants distribution, loan co-ordination, social services, economic development and settlement of inter-governmental disputes. In most of the new federations there are a number of institutions responsible for different functions, but in some cases many of them come under the jurisdiction of one institution as we find National Finance Council in Malaysia which is concerned with the distribution of taxes and grants with the loan requirement of the federal and state governments and with certain aspects of economic development and planning.

In almost all the federations some sort of review and grants allocation has been provided for and they are handled by the same Commission or Council. In India, a Finance Commission is appointed every five years in order to make recommendations regarding tax sharing, distribution of grants and any other matters referred to it in the interest of sound finance. Under the 1956 Pakistan Constitution, the National Finance Commission was to meet every five years in order to make recommendations regarding the sharing of taxes, grants-in-aid, public borrowings and any other matter of finance referred to it by the president. The Malaysia National Finance Council meets annually and must be consulted concerning grants to States, the assignment of portion of federal taxes to the States and any financial matters referred to it for discussion by the federal or State governments. In Nigeria, there has been frequent Review Commissions for example, 1947, 1951, 1953, 1958 onwards and on the recommendations of the Raisman Commission, such Commission are to become a regular feature. The Raisman Commission also recommended that another body, the National Economic Council, should include in its discussions consideration of those taxes levied by the federal government out of which the proceeds go to the regions. In the federation of Rhodesia and Nyasaland the first Fiscal Review Commission met in 1956 in order to consider the adequacy of the proportions of income and profit taxes and of export duties due to the territories and of the amounts raised by external borrowings and this Commission is appointed now in every five years. In the case of the West Indies here is no specific constitutional provision for fiscal reviews but this was to be included in the more general review of the Constitution. In some of the new federations, notably Malaysia and Pakistan the consideration of the loan requirements of the federal and State Governments is included among the functions of the Council or Commission reviewing tax and grant distribution. Nigeria with its Loan Advisory Board and Rhodesia and Nyasaland with Australian pattern of separate institutions deal with the co-ordination of federal and state public borrowing in India the states are not permitted to raise external loans and therefore no co-ordination body is considered necessary.

In most of the new federations there are also inter-governmental institutions to enable co-ordination of social services and economic planning. With the exception of Malaysia, the Commission and Councils dealing with social and economic planning and co-operation are distinct from these concerned with tax, grant or loan distribution. In India there is the National Development Council whose functions have been to lay down the outline for economic planning and to supervise the Planning Commission. In Pakistan, there is the National Economic Council to formulate financial, commercial and economic policy and to aim at uniform standard for economic development. In Malaysia, the National Finance Council includes in its functions, the consideration of development plans but there is in addition, the National Land Council, which formulates policy for land utilization in consultation with the federal and State Governments and the National Finance Council. The Nigeria National Economic Council was formed on the recommendations of the International Bank Commission, to consider development planning and to foster co-operation on and discussion on common problems crossing constitutional divisions. In the West Indies, a Regional Council of Ministers was set-up by the standing Federation Committee in 1957 to consider matters in the economic sphere of common interest to the territorial and federal governments. A unique inter-governmental device was the institution in Pakistan of Provincial Advisory Board for the federal posts and telegraph department. These boards in each province, consisting of federal and provincial representatives were charged with advising the federal government on the provincial operation of the federal department.

In some of the federations, special machinery has been provided to deal with federal State financial disputes not appropriate for Supreme Court jurisdiction. In Pakistan special tribunals appointed by the Chief Justice of the Supreme Court were given the responsibility for adjudication of inter-governmental disputes over costs incurred by delegated administration and over unreasonable federal restrictions on external borrowing by the provinces. In Malaysia Land Tribunals are provided for in the Constitution for the settlement of Inter-governmental disputes concerning payments for land and Special Tribunals are given the functions of setting disputes about financial compensation for delegated powers. The various inter-governmental financial Commissions and Board may consist of independent experts and government representatives. They may be advisory or regulatory. Among the group of Commissions consisting of independent experts, whose function is to consider the evidence impartially and arrive at an agreed recommendation are the Finance Commission of India and the Fiscal Review Commission of Nigeria. While they are empowered only to make recommendations, the tradition has grown generally that these should be accepted although there is no guarantee that this will always be so. The Special Quasi-judicial Tribunals for the settlement of financial disputes in Malaysia and Pakistan also consists of independent members but their decisions are binding. In large number of inter-governmental financial institutions in the new federations the membership is composed of representative of the federal and State Governments. In such cases the decisions are more likely to be arrived at through bargaining and sometimes voting takes place in which the State representatives may block central proposals. Such examples are the Malayan Land Council, the federation of Rhodesia and Nyasaland, the Pakistan National Finance Commission.

But at the same time, this arrangement provides an opportunity for exchange of views and co-operation. Where allocation of taxes and grants are concerned, the Advisory Commission of independent experts would seem more likely to result in a tradition of customary acceptance of its recommendations. The success of the Australian and Indian Commission is, however, encouraging on this point. One possibility that might be considered is a Commission composed of some or even all members from other Commonwealth countries, experienced in federalism, on a pattern similar to Reid Constitutional Commission for Malaya. In any case, impartiality is necessary.

### (g) Recent Trends

The second Finance Commission of India has noted certain recent trends in the federal-state fiscal relation in some of these new federations. In Nigeria federation, the distribution of revenue has been based on the principle of origin or derivation. Out of the Central taxes mentioned in the Constitution of Nigeria, as revised in 1954, the import duty on Motor spirit, half the import and excise duties of tobacco, one half of all other import duties, half the export duties, half the excise duty on beer, the proceeds of personal income tax and mining royalties were developed on the constituent units and distributed as nearly as possible by origin. This scheme of distribution was due for revision.

## Notes and References


1. The Gazetteer of India, Vol. 111, Ministry of Education and Social Welfare, Government of India, 1975, p. 927.
2. *Ibid*, p. 930.
3. A.P. Sharma: Prelude to Indian Federalism, Sterling Publishers, New Delhi, 1976, p. 243.
4. B.D. Basu, Introduction to the Constitution of India, Prentice Hall of India Private Ltd. New Delhi, 1980, p. 280.
5. *Ibid.*, p. 245.
6. *Ibid.*, p. 250.
7. *Ibid.*, p. 252.
8. R.K. Sinha, Evolution of Fiscal Federalism in India, p. 129.
9. *Ibid.*, p. 145.
10. *Ibid.*, p. 147.
11. P.K. Jha, Federal Finance in developing India, Capital Publishing House, Delhi, 1983, p. 30.
12. R.P. Verma, Federal Financial System in India, 1979, p. 73
13. P.K. Jha, p. 39.
14. *Ibid.*, p. 44.

# 3

# *Channels of Union-State Transfers in India*

## (I) NEED OF TRANSFER OF RESOURCES

Indian federalism imbibes the provisions of the American, Canadian and Australian Federations. These federations have increased their powers at the expense of the states. The political and philonsthropic ideals concentrated economic powers too. Indian Constitution has made the centre more powerful. This necessitates the transfer of resources from Centre to the states. The most striking reason to transfer the resources from centre to units has been the lopsided development of States. In search of speedier economic development the states need growing expenditure which they cannot meet out from their meager sources of income. Thus, in order to correct the interstate disparities scheme of allocation of resources become necessary. Dr. Varma rightly observed, "motivated either by the economies of distribution (the welfare ideal) or by the economies of production (economic growth objective) certain resources should be transferred from the union to the state and the system of such transfer should continuously adopt itself to the changing character of the problem of federal finance.[1]

## (II) CHANNEL OF TRANSFER

Broadly speaking, the channels of sources of income which are transferred from centre to states fall under three categories—Statutory, developmental and discretionary. Under the different constitutional provisions, finance commissions recommend the shares of the states into centre's income are known as statutory sources which are transferred or the advice of planning commission are termed as developmental transfers and grants of different ministries are called discretionary grants.

## Statutory Sources

The sources of transfer of resources from the Centre to the States in the Indian Constitution have been:

(i) Income Tax;
(ii) Union excise duties of certain articles;
(iii) Grants-in-aid in lieu of Jute Export duty (cessed at the end of 1959-60);
(iv) Grants-in-aid in lieu of revenues;
(v) Estate Duty on property other than agricultural land;
(vi) Tax on railway fares (now converted into a lump sum revenue grant);
(vii) Additional duties of excise (in lieu of Sales Tax on certain commodities);
(viii) Capital grants;
(ix) Loans; and
(x) Grants on account of Wealth Tax on Agricultural property.

The Constitution of India embodies three types of balancing factors. First, there are taxes levied and collected by the Union but assigned to the States (Article 269). The Union has the power to levy a surcharge for its own appropriation on any of these taxes (Article 271). There are also taxes levied by the Union but collected by the States (Article 2680).

Secondly, there is a provision for the sharing of taxes levied and collected by the Union. These are taxes on income (excluding Corporation tax) other than agricultural income and Union excise duties. These shared taxes are most important media of the transfer of resources from the Centre to the States.

Thirdly, provision for grants-in-aid by the Union to the States, are contained in Articles 275, 278 and 282. Under the substantive portion of Article 275, grants may be provided to States which are in need of assistance and different sums may be fixed for different States. The first proviso to Article 275 provides for grants in aid to the different States to meet the cost of such schemes of developments may be undertaken by the State with the approval of the Government of India for the purpose of promoting the welfare of the scheduled tribes in that State or raising the level of administration of the Scheduled areas. The second proviso to Article 275 provides special assistance for specified tribal areas of Assam of sums, capital and recurring, equivalent to (a) the average excess of expenditure over the revenues during the two years immediately preceding the commencement of this Constitution in respect of the administration of these areas.... and (b) the cost of such schemes of develonment as may be undertaken by the State with the approval of the Government of India for the purpose of raising the level of administration of the said areas to that of the administration of the rest of the areas of that State. Under Article 278, there is a transitional provision for 10 years from the commencement of the Constitution, authorizing the Union Government to give special grants to any part B State, if it is necessary to do so, as a result of federal financial integration. Under Article 282, the Union can "make any grants for any public purpose not withstanding that the purpose is notone with respect to which, parliament or the legislature of the State, as the case may be, may make laws". Grants under this head have been made for planning, subsidizing food prices, relief and rehabilitation of refugees, natural calamities, etc.[2]

### (i) Sharing of Income Tax in India

Sharing of Income Tax between the Centre and constituent units has become common in most of the federations of the world. But the distribution of income tax has formed a significantly larger proportion of the total annual transfers of funds from the Centre to the States in this country than in any other federations, like Austria and Canada, while in U.S.A. grants are usually the main vehicle for such transference of resources.

The sharing of income tax may take many forms. In the first place, there may be concurrent powers between federal and State taxes as we find in the U.S.A. and the West Indies. A Second device for income tax sharing has the common characteristic that the task of assessment and collection is unified and this method has been used in India where the federal government is obliged to levy and collected Income Tax and a considerable percentage of income tax proceeds are assigned to the States. An alternative method is to permit the States to add a percentage to the Central Tax for their own purposes. This is again found in Rhodesia and Nyasaland where the territories may levy a surcharge up to one-fifth of the federal tax. In the Scandinavian countries another method of sharing is practiced. Under this method income tax is in a sense treated as two taxes: (i) a proportional tax assessed on the first per cent of all income by the local governments and collected by them for their own purposes; and (ii) a surcharge falling progressively on higher percentages of incomes according to the Central Government.

In India, the framers of the Constitution being conscious of the imbalance inherent in the scheme of fiscal arrangements between the Union and the States, as envisaged in the Constitution, have provided under Article 270 for a mandatory participation of States in the sharing of "taxes on income". The proceeds attributable to the Union territories and taxes payable in respect of Union emolument as also any surcharge which may be levied for purposes of the Union are kept out of the divisible pool by virtue of the provisions contained in Articles 270(2), 270(3) and 270(4) of the Constitution. Taxes on income do not include corporation tax. By the amendment of the Income Tax Act, 1959, the Government of India decided to treat the taxes paid by the companies as corporation tax and this suddenly reduced the corpus of the divisible pool of income tax. Article 271 of the Constitution casts the responsibility on the Finance Commission to allocate the share of the income tax proceeds between the Union and the States.

### First Finance Commission

The recommendations of the First Finance Commission were available in 1952 and were given effect to for the five years ending 31st March, 1957. The Commission had to consider three matters:

- The percentage of the net proceeds of income-tax which should be assigned to the states;
- The manners in which the share so assigned shall be distributed among the states; and
- The percentage of the net proceeds which shall be deemed to represent proceeds attributable to part of States.

Regarding the percentage of distribution, the States Governments advocated fifty per cent to seventy per cent of the proceeds to be distributed among the States. Earlier in 1947, Sarkar Committee had recommended that the percentage of Income tax proceeds to be allocated to the States should be raised to 60 percent. The First Finance Commission felt that the share of the States should be increased from 50 per cent to 55 per cent.

With regard to the determination of the share of each State collection, relative population of each State, residence, relative Volume of industrial labour, relative per capita income, area, sparsity of population, economic backwardness, etc. were advocated by different States. After due consideration, the Commission accepted population and contribution as measured by collection as the basis of distribution.

Accordingly, the First Finance Commission recommended that 80 per cent of the stated share be distributed on the basis of population and 20 per cent on the basis of collection. Thus population emerged as the main criterion, because according to the Commission the main criterion of distribution should be the needs of the States and population gives a broad measure of need.

### *The Second Finance Commission*

The second Finance Commission was appointed in June 1956 under the Chairmanship of K. Santhanam. The states were unanimous in suggesting an increase in the percentage of net proceeds to be assigned to them though the percentage varied from 55 to 70. In view of the unanimous suggestions of the States, the Commission recommended that the percentage of the net proceeds assigned to the States should be raised from 55 to 60.

Divergent views were expressed by the States as regards the principle of distribution. Again population, origin, area, revenue needs, backwardness, collection, population of scheduled castes and tribes, etc., with varying weightage came up for consideration. The Commission found itself in substantial agreement with the First Finance Commission but held that "collection should be completely abandoned in favour of population as the basis of distribution". Inspite of its categorical declaration entirely in favour of population, the Commission did not want to cause a sudden break in the continuity and, therefore, proposed that the distribution of the States share should be 10 per cent on the basis of collection and 90 per cent on the basis of population. The Commission advised: "This should make it easy to complete, in due course, the process of eliminating the factor of collection altogether and distributing the entire amount on the basis of population." Besides, one per cent of the net proceeds of Income tax were prescribed as the share of Union territories.

### *The Third Finance Commission*

The Third Finance Commission submitted its report in December, 1961. All the States urged for substantial upward revision of their share. Some States even suggested that the entire net proceeds should be assigned to them. The Commission was not in favour of any drastic upward revision of their share. The Commission held that "in the case of divisible tax in which there was obligatory participation between the Union and the States, a sound maximum to adopt would be that all participating governments, more particularly the ones responsible for levy and collection, should have a significant continuing interest in the yield of the tax". The Commission felt that "it should be adequate if

66.67 per cent of the net proceeds of the tax be assigned for distribution to the States".

With regard to the principle of distribution, population, origin of collection, area of States, backwardness of the States and the proportion of Scheduled Castes and Tribes, all these familiar grounds were advocated before the Third Finance Commission. The Commission agreed that the relevant considerations are population and collection. But the Commission reverted to the recommendations of the First Finance Commission. The Commission hinted that even the Second Finance Commission which wanted population alone to be the criterion had observed. "There may be a case for weightage being given to collection in the restricted field of personal income tax. The First Finance Commission had gone further and stated: "It is pertinent to bear in mind the fact that there is all over the country a crore of income, which should be treated as a local origin". The case of collection became stronger due to the exclusion of company taxation from the divisible pool. Further, industrial states having large concentration of population particularly industrial labours have problems of law and order and an increased demand for administrative and social services. The Commission concluded: "we feel that it would be fair and equitable to restore the formula of the First Finance Commission for the distribution of income tax; namely, 80 per cent on the basis of population and 20 per cent on the basis of collection". The Commission fixed the share of Union territories at 2.5 per cent of the proceeds of income tax.

### *The Fourth Finance Commission*

The Fourth Finance Commission, under the chairmanship of Shri P.V. Rajamannar submitted its report in August, 1965 and recommended that 75 per cent of the net proceeds of income-tax in any year be distributed among the States. Almost all the States pleaded for a substantial increase from the existing level of 66.67 per cent. They argued that as a result of the change in the classification of income tax payable to the companies since the Finance Act 1959, the rate of growth of the divisible pool had been adversely affected. They also pointed out that while collection from the corporation tax had increased over six times in the last 12 years, the growth in the divisible pool of income tax had been less than 50 per cent. Some of the States reiterated their point that during normal times, there was no need for the levy of any surcharge exclusively for the Union and that in case a surcharge were levied, it should, as a matter of course, be merged with the basic rate of income-tax after a period of three years. The Commission, therefore, increased the States' share to 75 per cent.

Again, all the States placed various factors for distribution out of which only population and collection received acceptance by the Commission. The Commission was also of the opinion that a feeling of certainty and stability should be imparted as regards the principles governing the distribution of income tax. Accordingly, it retained the formula recommended by the First and Third Finance Commission for determining the share of each state in the divisible pool of income tax proceeds viz. 80 per cent on the basis of population and 20 per cent on the basis of collection. The Commission has also retained by applying the same principles of population and collection, the share of Union territories, in the divisible pool of income tax proceeds at 2.5 per cent.

### *The Fifth Finance Commission*

The Fifth Finance Commission submitted its report in 1969 under the Chairmanship of Shri Mahabir Tyagi. Most of the States suggested an increase in the percentage of the net proceeds of income tax to be assigned to the State, the suggestions varying from 80 per cent to 100 per cent. Some of them also suggested that the net proceeds to be divided between the Union and the States should include a part of whole of the proceeds of corporation tax and the surcharge at present levied on income tax for Union purposes or alternatively that the Union surcharge should be merged with the basic rates of income tax. The Commission felt that due to the shrinkage of the divisible pool on account of the corporation tax, the earlier Commission already increased the percentages in the net proceeds of income tax and hence there was no ground for the inclusion of corporation tax in the divisible pool. It further held that the Centre was within the specific provisions of Article 271 of the Constitution in levying a surcharge on income tax. As regards the size of the divisible pool, the Commission endorsed the view of the Fourth Finance Commission that Union Government must have interest in income tax and that percentage should be enlarged only when there is strong justification. The Commission concluded: "So far as the present five year period is concerned, he revised basis for determining the proceeds of income tax by including advanced tax collection without waiting for regular assessment has already resulted in increasing the size of the divisible pool so that the amounts which would be assigned to the States on the existing basis of 75 per cent would be larger. We do not, therefore, think it necessary to suggest any increase in the States' share of net proceeds."

On the question of allocation between the States of the percentage share assigned to the States together, seven States have suggested that it should be distributed wholly on the basis of population. Others suggested a weightage to population ranging from 50 per cent to 90 per cent with suitable weightage to other criteria suggested such as collections, areas, urban population and the States' per capita income. Only one State expressed the view that the existing scheme of distribution should not be reopened every time a new Finance Commission is appointed. The Fifth Finance Commission held: 'Considerable changes are likely to take place during the period between the appointment of two Finance Commissions in the economic and fiscal situation and the relative needs and resources of the States" and hence "there is nothing wrong in the principle in reviewing the basis of distribution of taxes by each Finance Commission". Therefore, the "Commission considered the matter *de novo*. The Commission examined in detail the question of granting weightage to contribution and discouraged it. The Commission concludes, "During the quinquennium from 1969-70 to 1973-74, 90 per cent of the State's share of the divisible pool of income tax should be distributed among them on the basis of population and the remaining 10 per cent on the basis of figures of assessment after allowing for reductions on account of appellate orders, refunds, revisions, rectifications, etc." The Commission fixed the percentage of each State according to this principle on the basis of 1951 census figure and further recommended that 2.6 per cent of the net proceeds of income tax be deemed to be the portion of such proceeds at attributable to Union territories.

### The Sixth Finance Commission

The Sixth Finance Commission has submitted its report in 1973 under the Chairmanship of Shri K. Brahmanand Reddi, former Chief Minister of Andhra Pradesh. Almost all the States have again pleaded before the commission for a significant increase in the divisible pool of income tax. Andhra Pradesh, Orissa and Punjab argued that the entire net proceeds of the income tax should be distributed among the States. Kerala proposed an increase in the share of the States to 95 per cent. Other States also pressed for argumentation of the divisible pool ranging from 80 per cent to 90 per cent. In justification of the further increase in the State's share of income tax, the States repeated the same ground that the permanent levy of income tax surcharge is against the spirit of the Constitution and adversely affects them. The States further urged that the corporation tax should also be brought within the divisible pool through an amendment of the Constitution. The Commission felt that in view of the explicit provisions of the Constitution, they all were precluded from recommending the inclusion of the surcharge on income tax for union purposes and the corporation tax in the divisible pool. But having regard to the near unanimity in the views expressed by the State Governments, they suggested that the question of bringing corporation tax within the divisible pool be brought up for consideration before the National Development Council.

As regards the States' share of the net proceeds of Income Tax, the Commission agreed with the earlier Commissions that the Centre which is responsible for the levy and collection of the income tax should continue to have a significant interest in it. However, they felt that there is a good case for a modest increase in the States' share of divisible pool of income tax. The Commission, therefore, recommended that the States' share of the net proceeds of income tax be raised from 75 per cent to 80 per cent during the period by this award.

Regarding the principle of distribution among the States of the percentage of the net proceeds of income tax assigned to them, the advanced States such as Gujarat, Maharashtra, Tamil Nadu and West Bengal pressed for a higher weightage for the factor of collection ranging from 40 to 50 per cent, the other states urged that the net proceeds of income tax, should be distributed wholly on the basis of population, some of the states also suggested weightage for other factors such as area, population of Scheduled Castes and Scheduled Tribes. U.P. urged that while 75 per cent of the proceeds may be distributed on the basis of population, the balance, of 25 per cent should be distributed only among those States whose per capita income is below the per capita national average. But the Sixth Finance Commission endorsed the concluded: "During the period covered by our award, namely 1974-75 to 1978-79, 90 percent of the State's share of the divisible pool of income tax should be distributed among them on the basis of population according to 1971 census and the remaining 10 per cent on the basis of figures of assessment after allowing for reductions on account of appellate orders, revisions, refunds and rectification". The commission further recommended that 1.79 per cent of the net proceeds of income tax may be taken to be the portion of such proceeds attributable to union territories.

### Seventh Finance Commission

The Seventh Finance Commission of India was constitution an order of the President, dated 23rd June, 1977 under the Chairmanship of Mr. J.M. Shelat, former Judge of the Supreme Court of India. The Commission made important departures in the statutory devolution of resources from Centre to States though the distribution of income tax does not manifest any change. Different States advocated different amendments in the distribution of income tax. The Commission increased the States' share in the divisible pool of income tax from 80 per cent to 85 per cent. The Commission decided that 10 per cent of the divisible pool of income tax should be distributed among the States in the same proportion of their contribution to the income tax revenue. For the purpose of determining the proportions of the contribution of the

States to the income tax revenue, it was decided to adopt like the last two Commissions, the State-wise proportions of net assessments taking the years 1972-73 to 1976-77. For the rest of the divisible pool of income tax, the tradition has been to distribute it in the population ratio of States. This is based on the theory that population is what the first Commission called "a broad measure of the needs of the States". Therefore, the Seventh Finance Commission decided that 90 per cent of the net proceeds of income tax shareable with the states should be distributed among them in population ratio. Thus the Commission, on the whole, recommended that net proceeds of income tax in each of the years 1979-80 to 1983-84 be distributed as follows:

(a) Out of the proceeds in each financial year, a sum equal to 2.19 per cent shall be deemed to represent the proceeds attributable to Union territories;
(b) The percentage of the net-proceeds, except the proportion representing the proceeds attributable to Union territories, to be assigned to the States, should be 85; and
(c) The distribution among the States *inter se* of the share assigned to the States in respect of each financial year was then fixed by the Commission.

### *Eighth Finance Commission*

In respect of the distribution of the net proceeds of income tax in each State the recommendation of commissions are as follows:

(a) The Commission recommended that out of the net proceeds of income tax in each financial year a sum equal to 1.792 per cent should be assigned to union territories. This percentage was, however, 2.19 under the recommendations of Seventh Finance Commission.
(b) At present, 85 per cent of the net proceeds of income tax excepting the portion representing the proceeds attributable to union territories, and the union emoluments is, distributed among the States. The share of the states is retained at the same level. It means that the Eighth Finance Commission maintained the percentage share of States of the net proceeds of income tax at the existing level, i.e. at 85% which was recommended by the Seventh Finance Commission. This percentage was eighty in the recommendations of Sixth Finance Commission.
(c) The Commission has also determined the share of each state from the divisible pool. It should, however, be noted

that the existing *inter se* distribution among the States of the net proceeds of income tax attributable to state has been partially altered by the commission. It means that the commission has partially changed the existing basis of distribution of the divisible pool of the proceed of income tax, among the States.

*Ninth Finance Commission*

(a) At present 85 per cent of the net proceeds of income tax excepting the portion representing the proceeds attributable to Union territories and the Union emoluments is, distributed among the States. This percentage was prescribed by the Seventh Finance Commission and was retained by the Eighth Finance Commission. Almost all State Governments have asked for enlargement of the state's share beyond the present limit of 85%, but the Commission was of the view that it would be counter-productive to increase the State's share beyond 85% as even now, the very small percentage share accruing to the Central Government gives it little incentive to raise the additional revenue from this source. Thus, Ninth Finance Commission recommended that, the State's share of income tax be retained at the prevailing level of 85 per cent of the net proceeds of income tax for 1989-90.

(b) The Commission recommended that, out of the net proceeds of income tax in each financial year, i.e. in the year 1989-90, a sum equal to 1.044 per cent of divisible pool assigned to Union Territories. This percentage was, however, 2.19 and 1.792 under the recommendations of Seventh and Eighth Finance Commission.

(c) The Commission has also determined the share of each State from the divisible pool for the financial year, 1989-90.

### (ii) Sharing of Union Excise Duties

Under Article 272 of the Constitution, if Parliament by law so provides, the whole or any part of the net proceeds of any Union Duties of Excise other than such duties medicinal and toilet preparations, can be paid out of the Consolidated Fund of India and distributed among the States to which the law imposing duties exceeds in accordance with such principles of distribution as may formulated by such law. Thus while Article 270 of the Constitution provides for a compulsory distribution of taxes on income between the Centre and the States, the distribution of the net proceeds of Union Excise Duties between the Centre and States is only permissive. None the less, successive Finance Commissions have recognized the fact that increasing participation of the states in the net proceeds of Union Excise Duties will alone bring about some degree of balance between their financial responsibilities in an era of planning and their resources. Ever since 1952-53, therefore, the states have been getting a share out of the proceeds of the Union Excise Duties.

First Finance Commission recommended sharing in respect of only three major commodities then subject to Union Excise Duties. In pursuance of the recommendations of successive Finance Commission, the share of states in Union Excise Duties has been progressively enlarged. By the time, the Fifth Finance Commission was set-up; the States were already sharing the proceeds of all Union Excise Duties excepting only special excise duties, regulatory duties of Excise and Cesses on commodities. The Fifth Finance Commission saw no justification for the exclusion of special duties of Excise from the divisible pool and recommended that they should be brought within the scheme of sharing from 1972-73. The levy of regulatory duties of excise has replaced under the Finance Act of 1973 by auxiliary duties on excisable goods. The Finance Act specifiscally lays down that those auxiliary duties have been levied for purposes of the Union and that the proceeds therefrom shall not be distributed among the States. But the Sixth Finance Commission has recommended that revenue from auxiliary duties should be brought within the divisible pool from 1976-77 onwards.

### *First Finance Commission*

Sofar as the distribution of excise duties is concerned; all the States except Bombay, Madhya Pradesh, and Rajasthan suggested the distribution of all the excise duties before the First Finance Commission. The Bombay Government suggested the distribution of duties on tobacco, matches, cloth, sugar and tyres, the Madhya Pradesh Government the duty on tobacco, the Assam Government the duties on sugar, cotton cloth and tobacco, matches, petrol and tea and the Rajasthan Government the duties on cloth, sugar, matches and tobacco. All the States except Assam, Mysore, Travancore, Cochin, Saurashtra (Gujarat), Punjab and Rajasthan proposed that the duties suggested by them should be distributed equally between the Centre and the States. The Government of Assam suggested that a sum of 30 crores of Rupees should be created annually for the benefit of the States from the proceeds of the duties on sugar, cotton cloth, matches and tobacco while excise duties on tea should be divided equally between the Centre and

States. In regard to the excise duties on petrol, the States asked for special allocation of 75 per cent of the duty to Assam on the basis of production. The government of Mysore and Travancore Cochin proposed that 70 per cent of the net proceeds of all excise duties should be allocated to the States, while the government of Saurashtra suggested that 60 per cent should be State's share. The Punjab and Rajasthan kept silent on this matter.

As regards the distribution among the States, Madras, West Bengal, Punjab and Bihar suggested consumption as the basis U.P., Madhya Pradesh, Assam, Madhya Bharat, Travancore Cochin and Pepsu proposed population, Orissa suggested that half the State's share should be distributed on the basis of the population and the balance on the basis of area of the States and Saurashtra suggested that 80 per cent should be distributed on population basis and the balance on the consumption basis. The Government of Bombay suggested the distribution of the State's share according to their relative contribution to the receipts. The Government of Mysore suggested that 45 per cent to 60 per cent of the State's share might be distributed on the basis of collection and 35 per cent to 50 per cent on the basis of population or consumption and 5 per cent with reference to special circumstances. The First Finance Commission recommended that 40 per cent of the net proceeds of Union excise duties on tobacco, matches and vegetable products be allocated to the States on the basis of their population. This percentage has been fixed with reference to the amount which should be transferred to the States by the division of excise duties. As a result of this recommendation, the Commission suggested the stoppage with effect from April, 1953 of yearly compensation paid to the States of Bombay (Rs. 54 lakh) and Madhya Pradesh (Rs. 15 lakh) on account of their refraining from levying tax on tobacco, but these States were freed to levy taxes on tobacco in the same manner as other States.

The selection of only three Union excise duties for division was on the ground that "the selected excise should be such as are levied on commodities which are of common and widespread consumption and which yield sizable share of revenue for distribution". The Commission's choice of population rather than consumption as the basis of distribution is mainly because of the unreliability of data regarding the consumption of each of the commodities in the various States. The Commission thus also fixed the percentage share of each State.

### *Second Finance Commission*

Before the Second Finance Commission, all States asked for an increase in the number of commodities the duties of which were to be shared. Bihar, Kerala, Mysore, Rajasthan, U.P., and West Bengal suggested the inclusion of all excise duties in the scheme. Orissa wanted the duties on sugar, paper, tea, and cotton cloth to be added; Assam, the duties on sugar, cotton cloth, motor spirit and tea, Punjab, the duties on sugar, cloth and tyre, Madhya Pradesh, the duties on sugar, kerosene, tea, cotton cloth, non-essential oils, and Bombay, the duties on sugar and cotton cloth, Andhra Pradesh, Madras did not make any specific suggestion but desired the inclusion of as many duties as possible or at least the duties on major articles. Jammu and Kashmir suggested the addition of duties on sugar, tyres and cloth.

As regards the State's share of divisible duties, Assam, Bihar, Bombay, Madras, Orissa, Punjab, U.P., West Bengal and Jammu and Kashmir suggested 50 per cent, Andhra Pradesh, Kerala and Madhya Pradesh 60 per cent and Mysore and Rajasthan 70 percent.

Suggestions were made also about the principles governing the distribution of the shares to the States. Andhra Pradesh, Bihar, Kerala, Madhya Pradesh, Madras and U.P. suggested population as the sole criterion, Bombay and West Bengal favoured consumption. Orissa proposed that 80 per cent should be distributed on the basis of population with a weightage for scheduled castes, scheduled tribes, backward classes and the rural population and the balance on the basis of area. Assam suggested the distribution of 80 per cent of the basis of population weighted according to area and the balance on the basis of origin. Rajasthan proposed the distribution of 80 per cent on the basis of population, 10 per cent with reference to the backwardness of area and 10 per cent on the basis of needs for developing the industries on the products of which Union excises are levied. Mysore recommended the distribution of 50 percent on the basis of population and the rest on the basis of collection. Punjab did not make any suggestion.

The Commission did not favour any 'sweeping change' by including all the excise duties in the divisible pool. However, they recommended the duties on sugar, tea, coffees, paper and vegetable, non-essential oils to be added in the divisible pool of Union excises along with the duties on matches, tobacco and vegetable products. With regard to the share the commission recommended 25 per cent and felt that the reduction in percentage from 40 to 25 on these commodities recommended by the First Finance Commission will be more than made good by the widening of the range of divisible duties and each State will receive a larger share.

As regards the principle to be followed in the distribution, the Commission observes that accurate statistics of consumption were not available and, therefore, they had to rely on population. But by such a position some of the States may be placed in a more advantageous position than others. Therefore, they recommended that "90 per cent of the State's share of the divisible union excise duties should be distributed on the basis of population the balance of 10 per cent being used for adjustment."

### *Third Finance Commission*

The States represented three alternatives before the Third Finance Commission. According to the States the distribution should cover the proceeds of Union excise duties on:

- article of common consumption,
- consumer goods, and
- all the commodities on the present list.

The majority of the States demanded that the entire net proceeds of Union excise duties should be made available for distribution. In view of the growing requirements of funds of the States the Commission agreed that the proceeds of all Union excises be brought in the divisible pool. The Commission, therefore, recommended "that 20 per cent of the net proceeds of Union excise duties on all commodities on which such duties are collected would be appropriate". The Commission accordingly included 35 articles on which excise duties were levied in 1961-62, excluding silk fabrics on which the yield was below Rs. 50 lakhs a year. They also excluded duties on motor spirit as they recommended that a sum of Rs. 36 crore being about 20 per cent of its yield should be distributed for maintenance and improvement of communications and distributed as special purpose grants.

With regard to the determination of State's share the Commission observed that "while population should continue to be the major factor of distribution, the relative financial weakness of the States, the disparity in the levels of development reached, the percentage of scheduled castes and tribes and backward classes in the population, etc. should also be taken into individually". The Commission, therefore, recommended that 20 percent of the net proceeds of the Union excise duties on the 35 articles mentioned should be distributed and fixed the percentage.

### *Fourth Finance Commission*

The States forcefully submitted for an expansion of the coverage of shareable excise duties before the Fourth Finance Commission. They argued that it was necessary to include in the shareable list all excisable commodities with a view to achieving co-ordination between the excise policies of the Union and the Sales tax policies of the States, ensuring greater evenness in the flow of resources, to the States and covering new products as diversification of the economic progress.

The Commission, therefore, recommended that 'all Union excise duties' currently levied (excluding regulatory duties, special excise and duties and cesses earmarked for specific purposes) as also those that might be levied in the next five year should be shared between the Union and the States. As regards the share of the States of the distributable excises, the Commission retained it at 20 per cent which made in effect amount of distribution 30 per cent and the Commission confined itself to the net proceeds of 35 commodities.

The Fourth Finance Commission made a departure in regard to the principles governing the distribution and recommended that the share of the States should be determined on the basis of 80 per cent on population and 20 per cent on economic and social backwardness as indicated by the per capita gross value of agricultural production per capita value added by manufacture, percentage of worker to the total production, etc. Thus, the Commission distinguished between economic and social backwardness of a State and its financial weakness, for according to the Commission "it is possible that a State may be economically backward and poor in social services and yet it may have a fairly comfortable position in revenue account".

### *Fifth Finance Commission*

In their memoranda submitted before the Fifth Finance Commission, the State Government have generally asked for an increase in their share of proceeds of excise duties from 20 per cent to higher levels ranging from 30 to 50 per cent,. One States had suggested that 30 per cent of the duties on petroleum products should be separately shared only among the States producing crude oils, the remaining 70 per cent being included in the general divisible pool. Another State suggested that at least 60 per cent of the yield from duty on Motor spirit should be separately distributed as a special grant to States which are backward in road communications. Many States have also demanded that the special duties of excise levied on certain articles in addition to basic duty which are now retained entirely by the Union should also be brought within the divisible pool and shared with the States. The States also pleaded that special excise duties should also be brought within the divisible pool.

The Commission recommended that the shares of the States should remain at 20 per cent of the divisible proceeds in each of the five years. It further recommended that the proceeds of special excise duties should be included in the divisible proceeds from the year 1972-73 if such special duties are continued till that year.

As regards the distribution of the State's share various views on the question were expressed by the States before the Fifth Finance Commission. Two States favoured continuance of the scheme laid down by the Fourth Finance Commission. Some States urged that economic backwardness is not a suitable criterion for devolution of taxes. One States has suggested that the distribution should be made on the basis of population and urban population so as to reflect the higher consumption in urban areas. Another States suggested distribution, entirely on the basis of consumption which may be measured by total sales tax collections. Two States have suggested that criteria should be population and per capita income. One of them suggested per capita income to be used for giving a share only to the States below the average level, while the other suggested inverse per capita income as the basis. Other States had suggested different weightage to be assigned to population and economic backwardness. One State suggested that all the three factors, population, economic backwardness and contribution should be given suitable weightage. One of the States expressed the view that the distribution should be mainly regulated by the financial needs of the States and some portion of the States share may be distributed on the basis of degree of tax effort achieved by the States, as an incentive. After considering the various proposals, the Commission recommended the distribution among the States on the following basis:

(1) 80 per cent on the basis of population of respective States.

(2) Out of the remaining 20 per cent.

   (i) 2/3rd should be distributed among States whose per capita income is below the average per capita income of all States in proportion to the shortfall of the States per capita income from all States average multiplied by the population of the State. For this purpose Nagaland for which the requisite per capita income statistics were not available should be equated with Assam.

   (ii) 1/3rd should be distributed according to the integrated index of backwardness on the basis of following six characteristics viz.

   - Scheduled tribes population,
   - Number of factory workers per lakh population,
   - Net irrigated area per cultivator,
   - Length of railways and surfaced roads per 100 square kilometres,
   - Shortfall in number of school going children as compared to those of school going age, and
   - Number of hospital beds per 1000 population.

According to the Fifth Finance Commission recommended that during each of the years 1969-70 to 1971-72 a sum equivalent to 20 per cent of the net proceeds of Union duties of excise on all articles levied and collected in the respective year, including special excise but excluding regulatory duties and cesses levied under special Acts and earmarked for special purposes, should be paid out of the Consolidated Fund of India to the States and the Commission fixed the percentages.

### *Sixth Finance Commission*

As the buoyancy of Union Excise duties in recent years has been significantly higher than that of income tax, all the States except Assam pressed before the sixth Finance Commission for augmentation of the divisible pool of Union excise duties. Some of the States, Andhra Pradesh, Kerala, Punjab, Tamil Nadu, Uttar Pradesh and West Bengal have suggested enhancement of the State's share of Union Excise duties from the present level of 20 per cent to 50 per cent. Others have urged increase ranging from a minimum of 33.5 percent to 40 percent. The Commission felt that the State's share of all basic the duties of excise should be retained at 20 per cent during the period covered by its award. Twenty per cent of the net proceeds of auxiliary duties of excise shall also be shareable from 1976-77 onwards.

While there was near unanimity among the States in demanding an increase in the share of Union Excise Duties there were wide divergences in their approach to the principles of determination of the relative shares of the States in the divisible pool. Each state was obliged to put forward a formula that would favour it most. Andhra Pradesh and Haryana urged distribution wholly on the basis of population while Maharashtra and Tamil Nadu Pleaded for weightage for urban and rural population in the ratio of 30:70. West Bengal also pressed for population as the sole relevant factor but with weightage of 40 per cent for urban population. Assam, Bihar and Nagaland favoured continuation of the existing arrangements namely, 80 per cent on population and 20 per cent on the basis of per capita income and index of backwardness. Gujarat argued in favour of distribution of 80 percent on the basis of population to Sales tax collections, Kerala put forward an altogether new approach in proposing distribution on the basis of population and budgetary needs with equal weightage for both. Mysore contented that the entire distribution of Tax proceeds should be treated as one unit and allocated among the States 90 per cent on the basis of population and 10 per cent on the basis of development index or relative per capita income. U.P. urged that 75 per cent of the divisible pool should be distributed on the basis of population and the remaining 25 per cent only among the States whose per capita income is below national average in the inverse ratio of the per capita income. Madhya Pradesh, Meghalaya, Orissa, Rajasthan and Tripura urged that apart from backwardness and population, certain other facts such as percentage of scheduled castes and scheduled tribes should also be deemed relevant to the distribution of Union excise duties. The State, on the whole, suggested more than 22 criteria for the distribution of excise duties.

The Commission accepted population and per capita income as the basis of distribution of Union excise duties. The Commission recommended that while the weightage for backwardness should be raised from 20 per cent to 25 percent the interstate distribution of this portion of Union excise duties should be in relation to the distance of a State's per capita income from that of the State with the highest per capita income multiplied by the population of the State concerned according to 1971 census. The balance of 75 per cent of the State's share of the divisible pool of Union excise duties should be distributed on the basis of population of the States according to 1971 census.

The Commission finally recommended:

(a) During each of the years 1974-75 and 1975-76, a sum equivalent to 20 per cent of the net proceeds of Union duties of excise on all articles levied and collected in that year excluding auxiliary duties of excise and cesses levied under special Acts and earmarked for special purposes should be paid out of the Consolidated Fund of India to the States.

(b) During the years 1976-77, 1977-78, and 1978-79, a sum equivalent to 20 per cent of the net proceeds of Union duties of excise on all articles levied and collected in the respective year including auxiliary duties of excise but excluding cesses levied under special Acts and earmarked for special purposes should be paid out of the Consolidated Fund of India to the States. The Commission than fixed the percentage.

### *Seventh Finance Commission*

In the distribution of Union Excise revenue, the Seventh Finance Commission appreciated the predominant role of the Union Excise duty in the transfer of financial resources to the States. The Commission recommended that the divisible pool of Union Excise duty should increase from 20 per cent to 40 per cent of the net proceeds of Excise duties. The Finance Commission felt that, the distribution of the net proceeds of Excise duties among the States be raised by the Finance Commission to make their contribution to the reduction of imbalances among the States. The Commission decided that the shares of the States in the divisible pool of Excise should be determined giving equal weight to the population factor, the inverse of the per capita State Domestic Product., the percentage of the poor in each State measured by a method which Prof. Raj Krishna has evolved for us and a formula of revenue equalization which we have worked out. Each of these principles has been given equal weight by 25 percent to determine the shares of the States in the divisible pool. The Commission, thus, recommended that during each of the year 1979-80 to 1983-84:

(a) The entire net proceeds of the Union Excise duty generation of electricity should be paid out of the consolidated Fund of India to each State in an amount equal to the collection in or attributable to that state; and
(b) Out of the balance of net proceeds of the Union excise duties levied and collected on all other articles excluding cesses levied under Special Acts and earmarked for special purposes, forty per cent should be paid out of the Consolidated Fund of India to the States and distributed among the States on the basis of the percentages fixed by the Commission.

*Eighth Finance Commission*

The Eight Finance Commission has enhanced the share in Union Excise Duties excluding excise duty on electricity from 40% to 45%. The Commission recommends that:

(i) The State's share in the net proceeds of shareable union excise duties excluding that on electricity should be 40%.
(ii) 40 percent of the net proceeds of shareable union excise duties, excluding that on electricity, should be distributed among the States on the basis of formula as given by the Commission.
(iii) The balance of 5% of the net proceeds of shareable Union duties of excise (excluding that on electricity) should be set aside and be distributed to those states which have deficit after taking into account their shares from the devolution, of taxes and duties as proposed by it. This introduces a new principle of directly linking devolution to deficits rather than dealing with them only through grants-in-aid under Article 275(1).

*Ninth Finance Commission*

The Commission recommended that:

(i) The State's share in the net proceeds of shareable Union excise duties excluding that on electricity should be 45%.

(ii) 40 per cent of the net proceeds of shareable Union excise duties, excluding that on electricity, should be distributed among the states on the basis Common Finance Commission. The Commission has assigned equal weight to State Finance Domestic Product and population in determining the shares of Individual States in the net proceeds of additional duties of excise. The Ninth Commission formula as given by the Commission.

(iii) The balance of 5% of the net proceeds of shareable Union duties of excise (excluding that on electricity) should be set aside and be distributed to those States which have deficit after taking into account their shares from the devolution of taxes.

## (iii) Sharing of Additional Duties of Excise

The Additional Duties of Excise (Goods of Special Importance) Act, 1957 was enacted in pursuance of a decision taken by the National Development Council in December, 1956 and the recommendations of the Second Finance Commission regarding distribution of the net proceeds among the States. Under the Act, additional duties of excise in lieu of Sales taxes then being levied by State Governments on Mill made textiles (except pure silk fabrics, sugar and tobacco) came to be levied and collected by the Union and the levy was extended subsequently to cover pure silk fabrics other than those manufactured on handlooms. The Act laid down the rates of duties chargeable on these items and also the schemes of distribution of the net proceeds among the States by way of payment of certain guaranteed amounts to each State and distribution of the excess by way of percentage shares. The Act does not debar the State Government from levying sales tax on the specified commodities but it provides that if in any year, a State Government levies a tax on the sale and purchase of such commodities, no shares shall be paid to that State in that year as its share out of the net proceeds of additional excise duties, unless the Government of India by special order otherwise direct.

### *Second Finance Commission*

The Second Finance Commission was asked to make recommendations with regard to additional excise duties on mill made cloth, sugar and tobacco which were being levied in case of Sales tax. The commission had to recommend the principles which should govern the distribution of the net proceeds among the States and the amount which should be assured to them as the income derived by them from the sales tax on mill made cloth, sugar and tobacco. After guaranteeing the present income for the balance the Commission has taken consumption corrected with reference to the population as the basis of distribution. The Commission recommended that:

1. In respect of union territories, 1 per cent of the net proceeds in any financial year of the additional excise duties on each of the three commodities being retained by the Union;
2. A sum equal to 1.5 per cent of such net proceeds be paid to the States of Jammu and Kashmir; and
3. Out of the balance of the net proceeds, the guaranteed amount of the additional excise duties and the percentage shares of the States were fixed by the Commission.

### *Third Finance Commission*

The Third Finance Commission just like the second Finance Commission did not accept the contention of the Sat that in determining the guaranteed amount, not only the current but also perspective revenue should be taken into consideration. In view of the fact that additional excise duties on silk fabrics in lieu of sales tax was levied and the yield from it was only Rs. 41 lakh, the Commission recommended that the amount of guarantee prescribed by the Second Finance Commission should be adopted with a small addition to take into account the yield from silk fabrics. The Commission recommended that a sum equal to 1 per cent of the net proceeds of additional excise duties be retained by the Union as being attributable to the Union territories and that the share of Jammu and Kashmir be raised from 1.5 per cent to 2.5 per cent a year. In respect of other States, the Commission fixed the annual guaranteed amount.

With regard to the distribution of amount remaining after the disbursement of the guaranteed amount the Commission observed that it would be equitable to distribute the excess collection partly on the basis of the percentage increase in the collection of sales tax in each year since 1957-58 when the additional duties were levied since additional excise duties were in lieu of the sales tax and partly on the basis of population. The Commission recommended that in addition to amount guaranteed, the States should participate in the distribution of collections in excess of amounts so provided and fixed the ratio.

### *Fourth Finance Commission*

The Fourth Finance Commission was required to determine the basis for distribution of additional amount over and above the guaranteed amount of additional excise duties. The Fourth Finance Commission considered that collection of sales tax in State is a more direct indicator of the contribution made by each state to the divisible surplus than population and accordingly recommended that excess over the guaranteed amount may be assigned on the basis of proportion of the sales tax revenue realized in each State to the total sales tax collections in all the States revenue together over the years 1961-62 and 1963-64. As regards Jammu and Kashmir which had no sales tax in 1957-58, the Commission recommended one and a half per cent. The Fourth Finance Commission, in sum, has recommended that out of the net proceeds of additional excise duties in lieu of sales tax for the years 1966-67, to 1971 one percent can be assigned to Union territories, 1.5 per cent be paid to the States of Jammu and Kashmir .05 of one per cent to be paid to the State of Nagaland and of the balance (97.5 per cent) of the net proceeds, the guaranteed amount of Rs. 3254 lakh be set apart and the rest distributed on the basis of proportion which sales tax revenue collections in each State bear to total sales tax revenue in all the States over the years 1961-62 to 1963-64. The Commission worked out the detail.

### *Fifth Finance Commission*

Before the Fifth Finance Commission, a number of States suggested discontinuance of the scheme but expressed willingness to agree to its continuance if certain modifications were made so as to enhance the yield from the additional excise duties adequately. Some of them suggested for this purpose that the rates of duties should be directly related to the rates of basic and special excise duties. While other States suggested that may be reviewed so as to reflect the increase in the prices of the commodities in question and the average income of States sales taxes on smaller items. About half the number of States urged that the existing arrangements should be discontinued and they are allowed to levy sales tax on the commodities themselves. They were not in favour of continuing the scheme even if modifications were made to increase the rates of duty. The Commission recommended that the Government of India should discuss the matter further with the States and continue the scheme if at all with suitable modifications.

Regarding the guaranteed amount, the Commission did not make any change except that it worked out the shares of the new States of Punjab and Haryana on the basis of the amount guaranteed to the former Punjab State. The Commission determined the share of Kashmir and Nagaland on the basis of population.

In regard to the principles for distribution the Commission felt that theoretically the best way of distributing the additional excise duties would be on the basis of consumption as approved in the agreement of the National Development Council. But consumption figures were not satisfactory. Considering that the excess of proceeds of additional excise duties over the guaranteed amounts should be distributed partly on the basis of sales tax collection during the year 1965-66 to 1967-68 and partly on the basis of population. The Commission accordingly worked out the percentage share of States on this basis with equal weightage to sales tax collections and populations. The Commission recommended that the net proceeds of the additional excise duties during each financial year should be distributed on the following basis:

(a) A sum equal to 2.05 per cent of such net proceeds is retained by the Union as attributable to Union territories.
(b) A sum equal to 0.83 per cent of such net proceeds is paid to the state of Jammu and Kashmir as its share.
(c) A sum equal to 0.09 per cent of such net proceeds is paid to the State of Nagaland as its share.
(d) Out of the remaining balance of 97.03 per cent, the Commission determined the guaranteed amount and fixed the percentage.

### *Sixth Finance Commission*

The sixth Finance Commission examined in detail the various aspects regarding the distribution of additional excise duties. Most of the States were now in favour of the continuance of the additional duties of excise. Gujarat, Haryana, Maharashtra and West Bengal desired that the excess of proceeds of additional excise duties over the guaranteed amount should be distributed entirely on the basis of the proportion of sales tax revenue realized in each State to the aggregate of sale tax collections in all the States taken together. Bihar, Himachal Pradesh, Madhya Pradesh, Orissa and Rajasthan urged that the excess over the guaranteed amount should be distributed on the basis of population in view of the absence of reliable data of consumption. Bihar also pleaded for suitable enhancement of guaranteed amount while Himachal Pradesh and Kerala did not want any reservation of guaranteed amount. Orissa urged that at least 75 per cent of the surplus available after providing the guaranteed amount and an appropriate share to the Union territories, Jammu and Kashmir and Nagaland, should be distributed in proportion to the population of the State. Assam pleaded for continuance of the existing principles. U.P. wanted the proceeds to be distributed in the same ratio as guaranteed amount of each State to the total guaranteed sum. Andhra Pradesh suggested that the revenue from additional excise duties should correspond to what the State could have got if they had the power to levy Sales tax. Jammu and Kashmir wanted that the growth of revenue of Sales Tax of the State should be a broad guide in determining the amounts to be allocated out of the proportion of general Sales Tax collection to consumption expenditure should be adopted as the base for distribution.

The Commission examined afresh the most equitable basis for

allocation. Theoretically, the Commission supported consumption as the most equitable basis. But the Commission found that available consumption figures cannot be regarded as providing equitable and firm basis for distribution of the proceeds of additional excise duties. The Commission rejected sales tax collection as indirect indicators of levels of consumption.

The Commission held that consumption is directly related to levels of income and, therefore, accepted latest available data on State domestic product as the broad indicator of the level of consumption. Population was considered to be the second determinant of consumption. Having regard to these considerations the Commission felt that population and the average of State domestic product for the three years—1967-68 to 1969-70 should be taken together as providing reasonable basis for assessment of the levels of consumption, population being given considerably higher weightage.

The Commission accepted the fixation of guaranteed amounts by the earlier Commission and made provisions for the new State of Assam and Meghalaya. The need to set apart the guaranteed amount and distribute the balance among the States and determined both of them together. The Commission finally formulated the principle that 70 per cent weightage should be given to population, 20 per cent for State domestic product and 10 per cent for production. The Commission recommended that the net proceeds of Additional excise duties during each financial year be distributed on the following basis:

(A) A sum equal to 1.41 per cent of such net proceeds be retained by the Union as attributable to Union territories; and

(B) The balance of 98.59 per cent of such net proceeds is distributed among the States in accordance with their respective percentage shares of such balance.

### *Seventh Finance Commission*

In the distribution of additional duties of excise, the earlier Finance Commissions recommended the principle for distribution of the net proceeds of additional excise duties among the States on the basis of consumption of articles in each State, since such a basis insured to the State's share more or less equivalent to what they have obtained, if they have continued to levy and collect sales taxes, before the Seventh Finance Commission, Gujarat, Maharashtra and U.P. took the position that the guaranteed amount should be first set apart as far as the principles of distribution are concerned. Andhra Pradesh and Assam have suggested no change in the formula of distribution adopted by the Sixth Commission. West Bengal has expressed no view Bihar has suggested that the entire proceed should be distributed on the population ratio of the States. Gujarat and U.P. have proposed distribution in the same ratio as that of the guaranteed amount of each State. Haryana has proposed that 10 percent of the proceeds should be distributed on the population ratio and the balance in the proportion of the sales tax in each State to the total sales tax of all States. Kerala, Maharashtra and Tamil Nadu have proposed the same basis as Haryana except that they would give no weight to population. Himachal Pradesh, Manipur and Meghalaya have discounted the sales tax collection criterion and have suggested weightage of 70 per cent to population, 20 per cent to backwardness and 10 per cent to production, while Manipur and Meghalaya would apply this formula to the entire net proceeds. Himachal Pradesh has suggested first setting apart 20 per cent of the proceeds for the hill areas which, according to it, consume these articles more than the plains. Nagaland has proposed weightage of 65 per cent to population, 25 per cent to backwardness and 10 per cent to production, while Punjab has suggested for the same factors, 50 per cent, 40 per cent and 10 per cent respectively. While Punjab and Orissa have both stated that consumption is the best basis of distribution, Orissa has suggested that the entire proceeds should be distributed in the population ratio. Rajasthan follows Orissa but has suggested as an alternative distribution of the net proceeds of the duties from the 3 groups of articles in proportion to the average consumer expenditure on each of them as worked out from the National Sample Survey. Jammu & Kashmir has pointed out that the growth in receipts from the additional excise duties has not kept pace with that in sales tax revenue of the State and has suggested that this imbalance should be corrected and the State adequately compensated in the sharing of the proceeds of the duties. Karnataka has proposed 90 per cent weightage to population and 10 per cent to backwardness measured by the distance of the per capita income from the maximum per capita income of any State. Madhya Pradesh has suggested a slight variation in these percentages, namely, 95 and 5. Tripura has proposed that 50 per cent of the proceeds should be distributed on the basis of density of population, 25 per cent on backwardness, 15 per cent on the basis of State income and 10 per cent on production.

The Commission agreed with the earlier commission that the appropriate basis for distribution is that of consumption in each state of the articles subject to the additional excise duties. As an indication of consumption the Commission adopted the data of the National Sample Survey 1972-73 (27th Round) of the Consumer expenditure.

### *Eighth Finance Commission*

Accordingly, the net proceeds of the additional excise duties during each financial year be distributed on the following bases:

(a) A sum of equal to 2.391 per cent of such net proceeds is retained by the Central Government as attributable to the Union territories. This percentage was 3.271 in case of the net proceeds of the additional duties of exercise on sugar and 2.192 per cent of textiles and tobacco under the recommendation of Seventh Finance Commission.

(b) The balance should be distributed among the States on the basis of equal weightage to State Domestic Product and its population. It means that 50 per cent of net proceeds of the divisible pool of additional excise duties is distributed among the States on the basis of the State Domestic Product, i.e. production and 50 per cent on the population of States. It should, however, be mentioned here that the basis of distribution under recommendations of the Seventh Finance Commission was State Domestic Product, i.e. production in the State in case of textiles and tobacco and the value of dispatches of each State in case of sugar.

### *Ninth Finance Commission*

The entire net proceeds of the additional excise duties on sugar, textile and tobacco excluding the portion attributable to Union Territories, accuse to the States. The Ninth Finance Commission has followed the pattern laid down by the Eighth Finance Commission.

Recommended that:

The net proceeds of the additional excise duties during each financial year are distributed on the following bases:

(a) A sum equal to 2.023 percent of such net proceeds is retained by the Central Government as attributable to the Union Territories. This percentage was 2.391 under the recommendations of Eighth Finance Commission.

(b) The balance should be distributed among the States on the basis of equal weightage to the State Domestic Product and the population. It means that 50 per cent of the net proceeds of the divisible pool of additional excise duties be distributed on the basis of population of States and 50 per cent on the basis of State Domestic Product, i.e. Production of the States.

It should, however, be mentioned here that, the basis of distribution under the recommendations of the Seventh Finance was State Domestic Product.

### (iv) Grants-in-aid in Lieu of Jute Export Duty

Under the Government of India Act, 1935, the net proceeds of the export duty on Jute products were shared with the provinces of Assam, Bihar, Orissa and West Bengal. The Constitution does not provide for the sharing of any duty of customs between the Union and the States but to enable these States to fill the gap of their revenues caused by the elimination of these receipts, provisions were made in Article 273 for the payment of grants-in-aid to them for a limited period in lieu of the assignment of any share of these duties. The period expired with the financial year 1959-60. These grants-in-aid were fixed sums unrelated to actual yield fro the export duty and although owing to the suspension of the duty and the ban on exports, the revenue has almost wiped out, these states have continued to receive fixed grants-in-aid.

Pending the appointment of a Finance Commission the question was referred to Shri C.D Deshmukh on whose recommendation the grants were fixed at Rs. 105 lakh for West Bengal, Rs. 40 lakh for Assam, Rs. 35 lakh for Bihar and Rs. 5 lakh for Orissa.

*The First Finance Commission*

The First Finance Commission didn't agree with the contention of the West Bengal that the amount of compensation of the grants should be related to the yield of the duties. In making their recommendations the Finance Commission used the year 1949-50 the last year in which the States were entitled to a share as the base year. In that year the net revenue from the export duty was Rs. 9681 lakh; at 62.5 per cent, the share of the producing provinces would amount to Rs. 605 lakh. In that year the quantity of raw jute exported was 2.01 lakh tons and the estimated quantity of raw jute used in the manufactured goods exported 8.38 lakh tons. Thus, the total jute exports were 10.39 lakh tons, against which the production of raw jute in that year in West Bengal was 2.59 lakh tons, in Bihar 1.29 lakh tons, in Assam 1.28 lakh tons and in Orissa 0.26 lakh tons. Thus, out of the total exports of 10.39 lakh tons, the jute grown in these States was 5.42 lakh tons. According to the commission, if their entire production of raw jute was used for export purposes, their proportionate share of the divisible pool of Rs.605 lakh amounts to Rs. 315 lakh.

This amount they have distributed amongst the four provinces in proportion to their jute production in the base year. Accordingly, the Commission recommended that the grants under Article 273 should be fixed at Rs. 150 lakh for West Bengal, Rs. 75 lakh each for Bihar and Assam and Rs. 15 lakh for Orissa.

The Second Finance Commission held that the amounts

mentioned in their interim report which are equal to the sums prescribed on the recommendations of the First Finance Commission, as subsequently readjusted on account of the transfer of certain areas from Bihar to West Bengal should continue till the grants automatically cease at the end of the Financial Year, 1969-70. They accordingly recommended that the sums to be prescribed under Article 273 be as follows:

Assam: 75 lakh, Bihar: 72.31 lakh, Orissa: 15 lakh and West Bengal: 152.69 lakh.

### (v) Distribution of Estate Duty

Under Article 269 of the Constitution, estate duty on property other than agricultural land is to be levied and collected by the Union, but the net proceeds except the proceeds attributable to Union Territories have to be assigned to the States and distributed among them in accordance with the principle formulated by the law of parliament. Estate Duty was first levied in this country in 1953 and the total collection upto 31st March, 1957 have amounted to Rs. 4.3/4 crore. Pending Parliamentary legislation, the net proceeds have been provisionally distributed among the States in the same ratio as the States' share of the divisible pool of Income-Tax.

#### *Second Finance Commission*

A variety of suggestions were made by the States in regard to the principle of distribution before the Second Finance Commission. Andhra Pradesh, Bihar, Kerala, Punjab and Uttar Pradesh proposed population as the suitable basis. Mysore suggested that 90 percent should be allocated on the basis of population and 10 per cent on the basis of collection, Madhya Pradesh half by population and half in proportion to the population of scheduled castes and scheduled tribes, and Orissa 20 per cent on the basis of area and the balance on the basis of population with a weightage for scheduled castes, scheduled tribes and backward classes. Assam wanted the proportion attributable to immoveable property to be distributed by location and balance on the principles adopted for the distribution of Income tax while Madras favoured distribution in the same proportion as Income Tax. West Bengal was for distribution on the basis of attributes and Bombay on the basis of collection. Rajasthan proposed that 80 per cent should be distributed on the basis of population and 10 per cent on the basis of backwardness and revenue needs, the balance of 10 percent being reserved for border States. Jammu and Kashmir wanted the distribution to be half on the basis of population and half on the basis of area.

The Second Finance Commission felt that estate duty being a tax on property, the basis of location would be the most appropriate principle of distribution. It was considered not possible to apply this principle in the case of the part relating to moveable property which may be included in an estate and in respect of it some general principle of distribution such as population is inescapable. The Commission, therefore, recommended:

- That out of the net proceeds of the duty in any financial year a sum equal to 1 per cent be retained by the Union as proceeds attributable to Union territories.
- The balance be apportioned between immovable property and other property in the ratio of the gross value of all such properties brought into assessment in that year.

The sum thus apportioned to the immovable property be distributed among the States in proportion to the gross value of the immovable property located in each State, the sum apportioned to the property be distributed among the States in proportion to their population.

### *Third Finance Commission*

The Third Finance Commission did not propose any change in the principle enunciated by the Second Finance Commission with regard to the principle of distribution and fixed the percentages for different States.

### *Fourth Finance Commission*

The Fourth Finance Commission recommended the continuance of the principle of distribution of the estate duty already laid down by the Second Commission and accepted by the Third Commission also namely that the part of the proceeds arising from immovable property should be distributed among the States on the basis of location and the rest should be distributed among the States in proportion to their population. The only departure made was that the share of the Union Territories was raised from 1 per cent to 2 per cent of the net proceeds.

### *Fifth Finance Commission*

Before the Fifth Finance Commission, some State Governments suggested that the distribution should be made on the basis of relative needs, population and collection. But the Commission has not favoured any change in the principle of distribution of estate duty. The Commission in interim report has recommended one per cent increase in the share of Union territories raising it to three per cent taking into account the rise in population of Union territories and gross value of immoveable property brought under assessment during the quinquennium ending 1966-67. The balance of the net proceeds to be distributed on the principles recommended by the Second Finance Commission and endorsed by subsequent Commissions.

### *Sixth Finance Commission*

Most of the States were in favour of continuance of the existing principles before the Sixth Finance Commission. Some of them advocated criteria like population backwardness, location, collection, weightage for scheduled castes and scheduled tribes, inverse ratio of per capita income, etc. after considering the various proposals the Sixth Finance Commission observed: "We are convinced that the principle of distribution enunciated by the Second Commission and endorsed by all the subsequent Commissions do not call for any change.

With regard to the distribution of estate duty in respect of property other than agricultural land most of the States urged before the Seventh Finance Commission for the continuance of the existing principles of distribution. The Commission recommended that the net proceeds of estate duty in respect of property other than agricultural land brought to assessment in each of the years from 1979-80 to 1983-84 should be distributed among the States in proportion to the gross value of the immovable property as also property other than immovable property taken together located in each State excepting in regard to property located abroad. The Commission also held that the property located abroad imposed estate duty and the proceeds should be included in the share of the States where the relevant assessment was done.

### *Eighth Finance Commission*

The Eighth Finance Commission recommended of the continuance of the existing principles in regard to distribution of Finance Commission in this context, which are:

1. The net proceeds of Estate Duty in respect of property other than agricultural land attributable to Union territories should be distributed in the same manner and on the same principles as for the determination of the shares of the each State, taking, the union territories as one unit for the purpose;
2. The balance of the net proceeds of Estate Duty in each year should be distributed among the States in proportion to the gross value of the immovable property and property other than immovable taken together located in each state and brought into assessment. As for property located abroad, it should be deemed to be located in the State, where it is brought to assessment; and

3. Sikkim will also be entitled to share in the net proceeds of this duty, calculated in the same manner as for other State, as from the date duty may become leviable in that State in the period covered by the report.

*Ninth Finance Commission*

The Ninth Finance Commission has followed the pattern laid down by the Eighth Finance Commission.

Recommended that:

The net proceeds of the additional excise duties during each financial year be distributed on the following bases:

(a) A sum equal to 2.023 per cent of such net proceeds be retained by the Central Government as attributable to the Union Territories. This percentage was 2.301 under the recommendations of Eighth Finance Commission.

(b) The balance should be distributed among the States on the basis of equal weightage to the State Domestic Product and the population.

## (vi) Distribution of Tax on Railway Passenger Fares

Tax on railway passenger fares was among the category of taxes which were levied and collected by the Union but assignable to the States in terms of Article 269(d) of the constitution. A tax on the railway passenger fares was for the first time levied under the provision of the Railway Passenger Fares Tax Act, 1956.

*Second Finance Commission*

The Second Finance Commission was asked to go into the principles which should govern the distribution of the net proceeds of the Tax among the States. In formulating its recommendations in this regard, some States recommended population as the basis; others wanted the needs of the States in addition to population to be taken into consideration, while some suggested earning from Passenger Fares area of the State, collection and weightage for scheduled castes and scheduled tribes as the criteria. The Commission was guided by the Cardinal principle that each State should be enabled to get as nearly as possible the share of the net proceeds on account of the actual passenger travel in railways within its limits. In its judgment this objective could be secured by allocating the passenger earnings from non-suburban services for each gauge of each railway zone separately among the States covered by it according to the route length following within each State. On the basis of the average recent earnings and expressing it as fixed percentages applicable for five years from 1957-58 the Commission fixed the percentages for various States.

Though the recommendations of the Second Finance Commission were to hold good till 1961-62, the Railway Passenger Fares Act was repeated in 1961 and the tax was merged in the basis fare with effect from 1st April, 1961 in pursuance of the recommendations of the Railway Convention Committee before whom the Railway Board had urged that the levy of the Passengers Fares tax had limited the scope for raising passenger fares. Though the levy on passenger fares was then given up, the Government of India decided to make an *ad-hoc* grant of Rs. 12.5 crore a year to States in lieu of the tax for a period of five years from 1961-62 to 1965-66. This grant was later raised to Rs. 16.25 crore from 1966-67 and has since then continued at the same level.

### *The Third, Fourth and Fifth Finance Commissions*

These Commissions which were asked to deal with the distribution of these *ad-hoc* grants were of the view that it should be on the principle of compensation so as to place the States broadly on the same footing that prevailed prior to the repeal of the Act. Accordingly, the grant is being distributed with reference to the share of each States as arrived at by allocating the passenger earnings of each railway zone on the basis of the actual route length in each State.

### *Sixth Finance Commission*

Before the Sixth Finance Commission, most of the State Governments were in favour of continuance of the existing principle without any change. But almost all the States made a vehement plea against the grant being frozen at Rs. 16.25 crore per year and have urged that the Commission should recommend to the Government of India enhancement of the grant *pari-pasu* with the increase in earnings from passenger fares. The Commission was impressed with the arguments. The States also argued that the present arrangement is inequitable and against the spirit of the Constitution as it deprives the States of the access to the modest share of the growing revenues of the Railways which the Constitution assigned.

The Commission urged: "The Government of India should re-determine the amount of grant payable in lieu of a tax on passenger fares in terms of what the State could have got if the Railways Passenger Fares Tax had continued in its original form. The additional loss to the Centre or gain to the States may only be of a marginal nature. But it will have a significant favourable impact on the Centre-State financial relations". Regarding the principle of distribution, the Sixth Finance Commission observed: "The existing principles of distribution which are substantially the same as those formulated by the Second Finance Commission have stood the test of time. In the continuing absence of statistics on passenger earnings in each State on account of actual travel within its limits, the allocation of passenger earnings from non-suburban services from each gauge for each railway zone separately among the States according to route length lying within each State would be the most equitable basis for distribution of the grant".

### Seventh Finance Commission

The Third, Fourth and Fifth Finance Commission which have been asked to deal with the distribution of this *ad-hoc* grant to the States, i.e. grant in lieu of tax in Railway passenger fares considered that the principle of distribution should be such that the States will generally be in the same position in this matter as they were before the repeal of the Act. The sixth Finance Commission endorsed the same vied. The Seventh Finance Commission accepted the view that the basis for the distribution of the grant should be in the proportion of non-suburban passenger earnings in each state to the total passenger earnings in all the States by the provision of the Railway Passenger's fares ordinance 1971 formulated by the President in October, 1971.

The Commission was also of the opinion that the Government of India should specifiscally referred the question of increasing the question of grant in lieu of Railway passenger fares tax the appropriate Railway Convention Committee and estimated that the amount of the grant be enhanced to Rs. 30 crore a year.

### Eighth Finance Commission

The Eighth Finance Commission has recommended enhancement of the annual compensatory grant in lieu of repealed tax on railway passenger from present level of 23.12 crores to Rs. 95 crores.

As far as the basis of distribution is concerned, the commission recommended that the basis of distribution of the grants among the states be in the proportion of which the average non-sub-urban passenger earnings, attributable to a state bears to the aggregate average non-suburban earnings of all states of the year 1978-82.

Therefore, for the first time the states of Manipur, Meghalaya and Sikkim get shares in the grant in lieu of tax on railway passenger fares, though, they have no railway lines in their states. Their share will be determined on the basis of out-agency collections.

### Ninth Finance Commission

It was in 1957 that a tax on railway passenger fares was levied for the first time though the Railway Passengers Fare Act, 1957 to 31st March, 1961, when it was repealed by the Railway Passenger Fares (Repealed) Act, 1961.

The annual grants were distributed to the States in lieu of their share of the tax on railway passenger fares on the principle of compensation so as to place the States broadly on the same footing as they were before the tax was imposed. The existing scheme has been recommended by the Second Finance Commission which was adopted by the subsequent Finance Commission, i.e. which was endorsed by the Eighth Finance Commission also. Though the existing principle did not change but the level of grants in-creased in proportion of the railway passenger earnings had increased.

Thus, the Eighth Finance recommended enhancement of the annual compensatory grant of repealed tax on railway passenger fares from present level of 23.12 Eighth Finance Commission. Accordingly the Ninth Finance Commission recommended:

(i) The quantum of the grant in lieu of railway passenger fares tax should be retained at Rs. 95 crores for 1989-90.
(ii) The share of the States in the grant in lieu of the repealed tax on railway passenger fares be allocated in the same proportion as the average of the non-suburban passenger earnings in each states in the year 1983-84 to 1886-87 bears to the average of the aggregate non-suburban earnings all States in those years.

As far as the basis of distribution of the divisible pool is concerned, the Seventh Finance Commission recommended that, the divisible pool should be distributed in proportion to the railway traffic originating in each state.

### (vii) Grant on Account of Wealth Tax on Agricultural Property

The Wealth Tax Act had been enacted as early as 1957. Agricultural Property was exempt from the levy of Wealth Tax upto and inclusive of the assessment year 1969-70. The Finance Act of 1969 amended the Wealth Tax so as to extend the levy of Wealth Tax to agricultural property (except such property situated in Jammu and Kashmir) subject to certain exemptions with effect from the assessment year 1970-71.

Wealth tax is not one of those taxes or duties which under the provisions of the Constitution are to be shared with the states either on the obligatory or permissible basis. It was also not a tax levied and collected by the Centre and assigned in their entirety to the States as for example is the case with estate duty. However, when in 1969 agricultural land held by individuals and Hindu undivided families was made liable to Wealth Tax subject to certain limits, the Central Government decided that the net proceeds of Wealth Tax on agricultural land would be passed on to the States as grants-in-aid.

Under Paragraph 4(F) of the President's Order, the Sixth Finance Commission was required to make recommendations regarding "the principles governing the distribution among the States of the grant to be made available to the States on account of Wealth tax on agricultural property". The States suggested a number of principles governing the distribution of these grants. Distribution on the basis of location, collection, population distribution on the same basis as for income tax, distribution on the basis of population and partly on the basis of backwardness, distribution on the basis of rural population living below the subsistence level, distribution to make more fund available to agriculturally less developed State, etc. were the main suggestions advocated by the States. The Commission considered the relative merits of these suggestions carefully and came to a finding that Wealth tax on agricultural property is comparable in its incidence to estate duty in so far as the latter relates to immovable property. Accordingly, the Sixth Finance Commission has recommended "that the grants-in-aid to be made available to the States on account of Wealth tax on agricultural property should be distributed among the states in proportion to the value of agricultural property located in each State and brought to assessment in that year".

### *Seventh Finance Commission*

### *(Grants on account of Wealth tax on agricultural property)*

The Seventh Finance Commission suggested that in the circumstances we recommend that the share of each State in the grant in each of the years from 1979-80 to 1983-84 should be an account equivalent to the net collection in that State in each year. Sikkim will also become entitled to a share in the grant in accordance with this recommendation, if and when the levy of the wealth tax is extended to that state in the period covered by the report of the Commission.

### *Eighth Finance Commission*

The Eighth Finance Commission recommended that the share of each state in the grant on account of wealth tax on agricultural property should be an amount equivalent to the net collection in that State in that year. It would, however, be noted here that there is no change in the existing principles in regard to distribution of proceeds of estate duty and grant on account of Wealth Tax on Agricultural Property.

## (viii) Grant-in-Aid in India

In a federal system there develops disequilibrium between the financial capacity and financial need of the regional government. Therefore, "the grant is an effective instrument for bridging the gap between fiscal capacity and capacity for administration". According to

Thomas, "if property employed, federal aid will become an adjusting factor of great utility in the relations between the Central Government and the Units and will be a most valuable agency for ensuring a national minimum of economic welfare in the masses in this country". Except West Indies, there is provision for federal grants to States in almost all the federations. Aids, subsidies, subventions, grants-in-aid are the different terms used in different countries to indicate the help extended to the units by the Central or federal Governments. Aid is a term used in U.S.A. to indicate transfer of resources from the federal Government to the State Government to encourage expenditure on specific services; subventions is a term commonly used in France, Germany, Belgium and Switzerland. Grants- in-aid may take various forms viz.,

(1) Unconditional grants,
(2) Conditional grants with no matching requirements,
(3) Matching-grants-conditional grants with matching requirements,
(4) Compensation grants, and
(5) *Ad-hoc* grants.

Unconditional grants are more common in Canada. Australia and the U.S.A., unconditional grants-in-aid may be given in the form of fiscal sums determined (a) at random (b) with object of equalization and (c) on broad fiscal consideration. It may be given in the form of per capita grants at a flat rate or on varying rate usually equalizing. Conditional grants-in-aid is an assistance given by a federal government to a State Government with certain strings attached to them regarding services to be covered, advance approval of State plans and budgets, employment of personnel, specific standards, federal inspection, maintenance of accounts and records in a specified manner, periodical reporting and withdrawal of federal funds in case of waste negligence and unsatisfactory performance. Conditional grants are generally allotted on the basis of a flat sum of grants or discretionary grants unit allocations, or formula allocations. In U.S.A., Canada, Australia and many other federations such grants are used.

In India in the pre-1919 era, grants to provinces were a leading feature of financial adjustment. During the depression of 1930 and thereafter, Central grants to provinces were extended to relieve distress. The Bihar Earthquake of 1934 encouraged the provision for grants. In the pre-war era, grants from the Central Rural Development Fund for financing scheme of Animal Husbandry, agricultural research, Malaria control and improvement of small scale industries, etc. were made to the provinces. But the first statutory provision for grants to the provinces was made under section 142 of the Government of India Act, 1935. The Constitution of India provides for various types of grants viz., compensatory grants, grants for development of tribal regions, fiscal need grants and discretionary grants under Articles 275, 278 and 282 of the constitution as mentioned earlier.

## The Role of Grants-in-Aid

The grants-in-aid overcome State federal financial disequilibrium resulting from the constitutional arrangements and also help in correcting inter-state disequilibrium which results from regional heterogeneity. Sidney Webb is of the view that the units cannot be allowed to continue in a state of disease, squalor, ignorance or even bad roads. He recognizes that not only the affected unit but also the whole nation must bear the cost of such destitution since all are "member of one another". Speaking of the role of federal grants in U.S.A., the Report of the Congress by the Commission on Organization of the Executive Branch of the Government 1949 stated that "the plan of federal grants has development a division of responsibility; the National Government giving financial aid and establishing broad and standard, the State Government sharing the financial burden and maintaining primary responsibility for administration. In addition to decreasing inequalities of service, the grant-in-aid method has raised the level of all aid services without transferring functions entirely to the National Government. "The report of the Commission on Inter-Growth-mental Financial Relations in U.S.A. has pointed out that by the offer of grants-in-aid the federal government has been providing incentive to the States to take up new functions mainly in the field of social services and this has tended to equalize the conditions between poor and rich States". We discuss below the role of the grants-in-aid in a federal system:

### *(i) Imbalances between Sanctions and Resources*

In a federal system it is not found possible that each unit of Government should raise adequate resources for the administration and performance of function assigned to it by the Constitution. There develops a disequilibrium and lack of balance between the financial capacity and financial need of the regional governments. Therefore, the grants are an effective instrument for bridging the gap between fiscal capacity and capacity for administration.

### *(ii) Inter-regional Economic Disparities*

Federal grants-in-aid to States reduce regional disparity of governmental performance by improving the quality and quantity of governmental services in backward areas and by transferring public funds from the wealthier regions to poorer areas. The mechanism of grants also operates to secure the removal of wide disparities in the standard of social services and social conditions in the different States. In any federation, there are inter-state economic disparities in wealth, income level of economic development and standard of social services. Through the Central tax collecting and redistributing agency, the financially stronger States contribute through the medium of grants to the development of higher standard of social services in the financially weaker States and thus the level of social services in the economy as a whole are sought to be equalized and balanced.

### *(iii) Inter-governmental Relations*

Federal grants from the centre generally bring in its train central supervision; control and technical advice which help the units in the performance of their functions and at the same time cultivate spirit of coordination and mutual co-operation.

### *(iv) National Development Services*

In a federation there may be certain services of national importance which the units can perform but which they do not because of the paucity of funds or because of their disinclination to incur extra financial burden. Federal grants may remove these hindrances and may pave the way for the implementation of the programs of national importance by the States. It also encourages local participation and utilization of local minds and capacity to further the interest of national importance.

### *(v) Specific Tax Resources*

In most of the federations of the world there are specific tax resources which are reallocated through matching grants according to circumstances.

### *(vi) Losses of State Governments*

Grants-in-aid is an important medium for compensating the loss suffered by State Governments because certain taxes are federalized in which States have a vital interest or because there is any natural calamities or political upheaval causing financial loss. In India, grants in lieu of Jute export duty on Railway Passenger Fares and grants for natural calamities are the examples.

### *(vii) Inter-regional Equilibrium*

In a developing economy, the different regions may be at different levels of economic development. The more underdeveloped regions may possess enough potential resources requiring utilization. Therefore, federal grants may be directed towards the maximization of national production through the achievement of regional balance in economic development. The role of central grants in such cases is to supplement the investible resources of the backward States in order to secure inter-regional equilibrium in economic development. This leads to over investment in poorer States. As a result, there will be low productivity and stagnation of the economy as a whole. It will hinder the continuous flow of resources from less productive uses and the total national output is restricted in the absence of a balanced growth of the different States of a developing federation. The low level of income in the backward regions will not provide a sufficient margin for saving to foster the investment necessary for their development. Again, the level of output in the relatively advanced States instead of finding outlets in the low income areas will be limited by the level of consumption there. Therefore, their economic development will be retarded due to the lack of effective demand. To recall Philadelphia Charter "the poverty anywhere is a danger to prosperity everywhere". The grants-in-aid may operate as a powerful instrument to avert such a situation by promoting balanced regional development.

### *(viii) Flow of Resources*

Grants -in-aid may be used to dictate the flow of resources into different channels of investment in terms of the criterion of highest marginal productivity in order to accelerate the rate of economic development. In a planned economy trying to maximize the rate of economic growth it is necessary that the allocation of resources by the planning authorities be governed by the principle of equalizing marginal productivity in the different lines of investment. The pattern of investment embodied in the development plan has to be desired to confirm to the principle of allocative efficiency. The role of central grants in a developing economy is also to allocate resources in accordance with the criterion of allocative efficiency.

### *(ix) Budgetary Burden of Poorer States*

An important purpose of federal grants to State Government is fiscal with a view to helping the impoverished regions in their budgetary burdens in the performance of functions. In the absence of such a grant there would be a tremendous financial pressure on the meager resources of the financially poor States and as a result they would be compelled to place an undue reliance on regressive commodity taxes. There may be wide differences in the technical condition in different States and by federal aid favourable conditions are created and an opportunity is provided for the improvement of technical conditions in the administrative standards of the State Governments.

### *(x) Inter-personal Disparities in Wealth and Income*

The federal grants to States not only reduce inter-regional disparities in wealth and income but they also promote inter-personal equality of wealth and income. The Federal Government may also bring about a redistribution of income between the different incomes groups in the economy.

### *(xi) Cyclical Fluctuations*

The Federal grants to the Constituent units may maintain a high level of economic activity in time of deflationary gap and in this way it may operate as a counter-cyclical device to keep the level of spending by the regional government at a high level. With a flexible system of grant the quantum of grant may be reduce in a period of inflationary pressure and increased in time of depression.

### *(xii) Dispersal of Economic Activities*

Finally the federal grants to States can be used to correct the undue concentration of industrial and manufacturing activities in some units and contribute to a wide diffusion and dispersal of economic activities in the economy. Again, by promoting the economic expansion of financially deficit areas, grants-in-aid achieves a better inter-regional balance in economic development which is necessary for maintaining employment at high level.

## Distribution of Grants-in-aid in India

Article 280(3)(B) of the constitution casts on Finance Commission the duty of recommending the principles which should govern the grants-in-aid of revenue of the States under substantive provision of Article 175 of the constitution. In recommending grants-in-aid from Centre to the States, the First Finance Commission laid down the following principles:

(a) Budgetary needs,
(b) tax effort,
(c) economy in expenditure,
(d) standard of social services,
(e) special obligations, and
(f) broad purposes of national importance.

These principles have been considered unexceptionable by the subsequent Finance Commission. The First Finance Commission suggested that the budgetary needs of the States should be the starting point for determining the assistance required by the States, but that the needs thus disclosed should be adjusted with regard to certain other consideration. First, the budgets of the States should be reduced to a comparable basis by making adjustments in respect of abnormal, unusual and non-recurring items of revenue and expenditure. Secondly, the due allowance should be made for clear cases of failure of States to maximize tax efforts. Thirdly, in order not to pay a premium upon extravagance, the States' Endeavour to secure reasonable economy in expenditure should be taken into consideration. Fourthly, where standard of social services in any State are significantly lower than in others, it should qualify for special assistance. Fifthly, special disabilities of States due to abnormal conditions beyond their control should be provided for. Lastly, grants may be made to certain State for the furtherance of broad purposes of national importance such as primary education in respect of which they may be especially backward.

These principles have proved to be difficult in practical application. The principle of Tax Effort is "unexceptionable" but as the First Finance Commission admitted, it is only in clear cases of inadequate taxation that it should affect the quantum of assistance which the States may be otherwise qualified to get. Clear cases of inadequate taxation are difficult to determine. Low per capita taxation in poor States may simply be evidence of low taxable capacity. An agricultural State with a low level of purchasing power has to maintain a comparatively high level of per capita expenditure to sustain a reasonable standard of social services. An industrial State can raise much larger per capita revenue than the agricultural State even though the kinds and rates of taxes are same in both. It is, therefore, difficult to decide whether a State is taxing its people adequately in relation to their income and taxable capacity. Some kind of empirical judgment is inevitable.

The Second Finance Commission assumed that if a State raised additional revenue which it has promised for the plan, it will have done its parts. In facts, as Mr. Shastri remarks, "they have admittedly not been able to apply the criteria of tax effort and expenditure economy". The Third Finance Commission in this connection observed: "The earlier Commissions had rightly stressed the importance of efficiency and economy in administration and the tax efforts of the States. But they were unable to assess the relative efficiency and performance due to inadequacy and often unreliability of statistical and other material. With the limited time and organization at our disposal we would have been even otherwise unable to undertake either of these reviews and give recognition in our scheme of devolution to these States which had made the maximum effort in effecting economy in expenditure and raising resources. We have, therefore, been compelled like our predecessors to cover the annual budgetary gaps of all the states whether caused by normal growth of expenditure, the maintenance cost of completed scheme and mounting interest charges or even by a measure of improvidence". This observation also suggested for a permanent Finance Commission.

An important purpose of grants-in-aid is to help in equalizing the standard of basic social services. But the successive Finance Commission has also failed to achieve this objective. The Second Finance Commission observed: "It is the function of the Planning Commission and the National Development Council to ensure equalization as far as possible of the standard of essential social services in the various States of Unions. For our scheme of devolution we have accepted the plan as ensuring an equitable development in the field of Social Services. There is, therefore, now no reason for any grants in this field such as the grants for expansion of Primary education recommended by the last Commission".

### *First Finance Commission*

On the whole, the First Finance Commission in assessing the needs of a State and formulating recommendations in regard to the sum to be paid as grants-in-aid took into consideration the budgetary position of the States and the probable amount which would accrue to them under the devolution of revenue from income tax and union excises. They also took into consideration additional burdens arising out of the partition of the country in some States. They also kept in view the need for assessing to some extent the less developed States by the provision of special grants to raise the standard of one of the essential social services. In determining the eligibility of a States to grants-in-aid the Commission kept some broad considerations before it. First, assistance proposed by the Commission should meet the normal budgetary needs of these States and should allow a reasonable margin for expansion. Secondly, special problems created for some of the States by the partition of the country which have caused a significant addition to their expenditure should be adequately met. Accordingly, the First Finance Commission recommended grants and also special purpose grants for the development of primary education.

We shall reproduce the fiscal need grants recommended by the Commission in coming pages. The Commission came to the conclusion that Madras, Uttar Pradesh, Bihar, Madhya Bharat, Pepsu, Hyderabad, Rajasthan, Madhya Pradesh was not in need of assistance and, therefore, they were not given any assistance. As Bombay State was comparatively well developed, no grant-in-aid was recommended. The recommendations were accepted by the Government.

### *The Second Finance Commission*

The Second Finance Commission endorsed the basic principle of 'fiscal need', laid down by the First Finance Commission as "unexceptionable" although its emphasis on these principles were influenced by the development which had subsequently taken place. The Commission interpreted "Fiscal need" comprehensively by taking into account the impact of the completion of the First Five Year Plan and the needs of the Second Plan. It took an integrated view of the Finance of the Centre and the States and the financial capacity of the Union to assist the States after meeting its own essential commitments. Therefore, it attempted to formulate a scheme of grants-in-aid which should normally enable the States to balance their budgets after meeting their normal revenue expenditure as well as the revenue expenditure incidental to the implementation of the Second Five Year Plan.

In estimating the fiscal need and fiscal capacity of the States, the Commission reduces the State budgets to a comparable basis and allowed for various factors by which the computation of budgetary needs had to be adjusted. In addition, the Commission treated grants-in-aid as residuary assistance to the States after taking into account devolution of revenue in other forms. In measuring the tax efforts as suggested by the First Finance Commission, the Second Finance Commission assumed that if a State raised additional revenue which it had promised for the plan it will have done its part. An important principle stressed by the First Finance Commission was that the grants-in-aid should be utilized in reducing inequalities in the standards of basic social services in the States. But the Second Finance Commission did not recommend any Special grants for the equalization of the standard of social services and it left it to be the Planning Commission and the National Development Council to measure the equalization. Thus, the Commission recommended following principles which should govern the extent of federal grants to States:

"(1) The eligibility of a State to grants-in-aid and the amount of such aid should depend upon its fiscal need in a comprehensive sense. In a Union in which the Centre and the States co-operate for a planned development, grants-in-aid should sub-serve this end. Priorities and provisions in the plan itself should determine the fiscal needs for development for the period of the plan,

(2) The gap between the ordinary revenue of a State and its normal inescapable expenditure should as far as possible be used by sharing of taxes; grants-in-aid should be largely a residuary form of assistance given in the form of general and unconditional grants, and

(3) Grants for broad purposes may also be given. While they

> last they should be grant-in-aid of revenues, but the state would be under an obligation to spend the whole amount in furtherance of the board purposes indicates. Where the purposes are provided for in a comprehensive plan, there will be no scope for such grants."

The main objective of Second Finance Commission in this respect has been "to ensure that the States have sufficient revenues to meet normal expenditure and their commitments in respect of the plan expenditure on revenue accounts". On these principles the Second Finance Commission recommended grants-in-aid to the States the amount of which was much larger. The total grants-in-aid recommended by the Second Finance Commission came to Rs. 187.7 crore. The Commission came to the conclusion that Bombay, Madras and Uttar Pradesh were not in need of grants-in-aid as the devolution of revenue was sufficient to meet their current as well as plan expenditure. The other States were given grants-in-aid.

### *Third Finance Commission*

The Third Finance Commission felt that the principles laid down by the First Finance Commission with regard to grants-in-aid are "unexceptionable" in themselves but their practical application is difficult. The comparative determination of the tax efforts of the States cannot be in absolute terms. It has to be related to tax potential and these calls for a special study. Similarly, the measure of economy effected or the degree of efficiency reached in a states' administration is a complicated exercise which a Finance Commission with the organization and time at its disposal could hardly undertake. The Third Finance Commission agreed with the Second Finance Commission that fiscal needs should be interpreted in a comprehensive sense and that grants-in-aid should sub-serve the requirement of planned development. The Commission felt that "consistent with this concept of assistance to which we fully subscribe with accords also in our view, with the spirit and provisions of the Constitution, we should not live out of account consideration of the fiscal need of the plan. Our terms of reference also give recognition to this principle by directing specifiscally to take note of the 'Third Five Year Plan'. The Commission also felt that it was unscientific to draw a line on the basis of plan and non-plan expenditure and concluded that the entire revenue budget of a State whether plan or non-plan should be regarded as an integral whole. The Commission also suggested that;

(a) assistance which is meant to fulfil what can rightly be described as national purposes such as power, flood control, major irrigation works, agriculture, family planning, etc. should continue to be governed by strict conditions regarding their utilization; and

(b) grants which are meant to strengthen the State sector in matters which must necessarily be decided with the fullest regard to local rather than national needs, such as education, health, minor irrigation projects, etc. should be such that the States have the freedom to re-appropriate from one head of such allocation to another while adhering to the broad objectives of the plan.

In view of these facts the Commission recommended that the total amount of grants-in-aid should be of an order which would enable the States, along with any surplus out of devolution to cover 75 per cent of the revenue component of their plans. The recommendation to provide 75 per cent of revenue component of the plan expenditure as grants-in-aid was not unanimous as Shri G.R. Kamat, the official member Secretary in a dissenting note disagreed with the recommendation. According to him, the recommendation had serious impact on the concept and mechanism of National Planning and it is not likely to secure greater autonomy for the States on the plea of which the Commission took this step. The Government of India also did not accept the majority recommendation on the ground that as the grants for the plan schemes were already provided for under the plan, there was no need to impose rigid statutory obligation on the centre.

According to the recommendation of the Third Finance Commission, Andhra Pradesh and Orissa which were heavily in deficit received maximum grants. Bihar, Bengal, U.P., Maharashtra and Punjab received no statutory grants for matching the budgetary deficit. Besides, the Commission recommended a total sum of Rs. 36 crore for improvement of communications to be distributed among 10 States.

### *Fourth Finance Commission*

The Fourth Finance Commission also accepted budgetary needs as the basis for the distribution of grants-in-aid. The Commission excluded plan grants from the purview of its consideration. The Commission thought that there should not be any division of responsibility in regard to any element of plan expenditure and hence it did not think it to be appropriate to take upon itself the task of dealing with the States plan expenditure. The Commission did not recommended any special purpose grants either as it felt that their utilization cannot be effectively reviewed, however, it included certain special requirements in its forecasts of the expenditure revenue and expenditure of the States in the past and examined the forecasts of revenue and non-plan revenue expenditure for each State. The Commission decided to consider only those increases over present levels of expenditure which were based on firm decisions of the State Government and on which Government orders have been passed. In the case of these states, although firm decisions have been taken and government orders had been issued with regard to increased expenditure on certain heads, yet the Commission could not take them into account either because there was not sufficient time to examine them or because the proposals were not accompanied by the basic particulars and other necessary data. On the basis of the above factors the Commission worked out estimates for the non-plan revenue gap for each of the States for the Five Year period 1966-67 to 1970-71. The Commission also made estimates of the expected receipts of various central taxes likely to be received by the different States and concluded that the States of Bihar, Gujarat, Maharashtra, Punjab, Uttar Pradesh and West Bengal could have surpluses for the Five Year period. Hence, it did not recommend any grant for them. The remaining States were expected to have revenue deficits even after taking into account their shares of central taxes, and the Commission recommended grants-in-aid to them.

### *Fifth Finance Commission*

The Fifth Finance Commission analyzed the principles of grants applied by the various Finance Commissions and found that none of the Commissions could strictly apply these criteria. They further felt that "it is not possible for us to take into account any requirements for the Five Year Plan". In view of the rapid growth of State expenditure and very large size of budgetary deficits which, as indicated in the State forecasts, come to Rs. 7268 crore, the commission considered that "the emphasis must shift significantly from budgetary needs to broad fiscal needs as suggested by the Second Finance Commission". The Commission took into account the revenue receipts and tax-efforts, the States' revenue expenditures and economy consistent with efficiency into consideration and worked out the deficit and surplus of the States. The Commission came to the conclusion that in accordance with the assessment of the States' revenue resources and their requirement on revenue account for non-plan expenditure, the following States will, after the transfer to them by devolution of taxes as well as their share of the grant in lieu of tax on railway passenger fares and the proceeds of additional excise duties, have a surplus during the five years. The Commission did not recommend any grant to eight States, namely, Bihar, Gujarat, Haryana, Madhya Pradesh, Maharashtra, Mysore, Punjab and Uttar Pradesh.

### *Sixth Finance Commission*

The Sixth Finance Commission noted that all the earlier Finance

Commission have felt that grants-in-aid of revenues of the States should be related to the fiscal needs of the States and did not propose any change in the principle. It made a close and critical scrutiny of the forecasts of receipts and expenditure of State Governments for the determination of fiscal need. An important departure made by the Commission is a shift from "gap filling approach". As the Commission observes, "while we have made every effort to ensure the States adequate resources to maintain budgetary equilibrium, we have not adopted the approach of mechanical filling up of the gap between receipts and expenditure on present levels of efficiency in the collection of revenues and management of public enterprises". The Commission further says: "by far the most significant departure we have made from the approach of the earlier Finance Commission is in the process we have initiated of enabling the States that are backward in standards of general administration to come up to a certain national minimum. For this purpose we have identified certain administrative and social services as to be of crucial importance and have proposed that the States whose expenditure in per capita terms is below the all States' average should be enabled to come up to such an average by the last year of our award".

On the basis of the reassessment of revenue receipts and non-plan revenue expenditure of State Governments, taking into account the principles and general considerations and after setting-off the resources estimated to accrue to the States from devolution of taxes and duties and grants in lieu of tax under the repeated Railway Passenger Fares Tax Act, 1957, the surpluses and deficits of State Governments have been calculated by the Commission. In the light of all these, the Commission recommended that except Gujarat, Haryana, Karnataka, Madhya Pradesh, Maharashtra, Punjab and Tamil Nadu, other States of the Union be given grants-in-aid.

### *Seventh Finance Commission*

The Seventh Finance Commission examined the principles governing the distribution of grants-in-aid under Article 275 of the Constitution. A set of principles was adopted by the First Commission and these were broadly endorsed by the subsequent Commissions. The Seventh Finance Commission held that these principles were more in the nature of guidelines for interval work. The later Finance Commissions also had serious difficulties in the application of some of these principles, for instance measurement of the effects of economy and efficiency in expenditure assessment of the comparative tax efforts of the States. The Seventh Finance Commission formulated following principles for grants-in-aid under Article 275:

(a) Grants-in-aid may, in the first place, be given to States to enable them to cover fiscal gaps, if any are left after devolution of taxes and duties, so as to enable them to maintain the levels of existing services in the manner considered desirable as an in-built in their revenue forecasts. In this connection consideration should be given to the tax effort made by the individual States in relation to targets for the plan to economy in expenditure consistent with efficiency and to prudent management in public sector enterprises.

(b) Grants-in-aid may be made as correctives intended to narrow, as far as possible, disparities in the availability of various administrative and social services between the developed and the less developed States, the object being that every citizen, irrespective of the State boundaries. Within which he lives, to be provided with certain basic national minimum standards of such services. While the long term objectives may be to provide to each citizen these services at the levels obtaining in the most advanced States, due regard should be paid to the feasibility of upgrading these standards in the shorter term.

(c) Grants-in-aid may also be given to individual States to enable them to meet special burdens on their finances because of their peculiar circumstances or matters of national concern.

### *Eighth Finance Commission*

The Eighth Finance Commission found the existing financing arrangements of relief expenditure to be basically sound. It increased the combined annual margin money for the States from Rs. 100.55 crores to Rs. 240.75 crores. Besides, it also recommended that the Central Government should contribute by way of grant half of the margin money of each State. In this way, during 1985-89 a sum of Rs. 481.50 crores become payable to the States as margin money grants under the recommendation of the Commission. The Commission specified the mechanism as below:

(a) The following amounts of margin money per year be fixed for each State.

(b) The State Government should provide 50 per cent of the margin money mentioned above.

(c) The centre should contribute the balance of 50 per cent of the margin money per year as grants-in-aid.

(d) On the occurrence of a natural calamity a State will be entitled to draw on the centre's contribution after it has exhausted its own share of margin money.

(e) The State Government should make a contribution from its own plan outlay for providing relief employment. This contribution should not exceed 5 per cent of the Annual Plan out lay.

### *Ninth Finance Commission*

The Ninth Finance Commission made grants-in-aid to cover revenue gap (i.e. the gap between revenue receipts and revenue expenditure), (2) and grants-in-aid for revenue plan, (3) grants-in-aid for upgradations, (4) grants-in-aid to special problems of the States, (5) grants-in-aid for the balance of works under special problems for which grants were recommended by the Eighth Finance Commission, and (6) Centre's contribution as margin money to the States.

## Transfer for Resources through Finance Commission in India

The Finance Commission determines share of States in the net yield from Income-Tax, Union Excise Duties, Grants-in-aid in lieu of Jute Export Duty, and Grants under Article 275 of the constitution. Estate Duty on property other than agriculture and agricultural property, tax on Railway Passenger Fares converted into lump sum revenue grants, Additional Duties of Excise in lieu of Sales Tax on certain commodities and Grants on account of Wealth Tax on agricultural property.

The transfer of resources on the recommendation of the First Finance Commission doubled in the award of Second Finance Commission which again doubled in the Fourth Finance Commission. The award of three times more under the Fifth Finance Commission it received 9.57 per cent of the total devolution and under Sixth Finance Commission, it received 8.79 per cent. Bihar has been refused grants under Article 275 five times by the First, Third, Fourth, Fifth and Seventh Finance Commissions. The transfer of resources by the Finance Commissions from Centre to Bihar has invariably been lower than the national average in per capita terms. Similar is the case with some of the middle spectrum States like Uttar Pradesh, Tamil Nadu, Gujarat, Madhya Pradesh, Karnataka and lower spectrum States of Rajasthan. However, the Seventh Finance Commission of India has tilted the balance in favour of low spectrum and middle Spectrum of States' income.

### *Seventh Finance Commission and Underdeveloped States—A Case Study of Bihar*

The report of the Seventh Finance Commission has been received with mixed reactions. It has unanimously made major progressive innovations in many aspects of the traditional schemes of resource transfer to the States. It has recommended a record amount of overall devolution from the Centre to the States. It has doubled the proportion of shareable excise revenue given to the States from 20 to 40 per cent and increased the share of States in the divisible pool of income tax from 80 to 85 per cent. Thus, the total devolution is more than twice the devolution by the Sixth Finance Commission. It has liberalized and rationalized general expenditure forecasts and earmarked provisions on account of relief expenditure, debt relief, increase in the emolument of State Government employees and upgradations of the Standard of public services.

In a growth-oriented federal structure, Federal Finance must operate to secure the objectives of federal finance, viz. revenue sufficiency; maximization of growth rate of the economy, and removal of inter-state economic disparities, etc. In India federal finance has not fully succeeded in achieving these objectives and the objectives of equity in the sense of adequate flow of funds to the poor States to compensate for their deficiencies in fiscal capacity, thus yet remains to be achieved.

In the field of Plan-assistance the Gadgil Formula also failed to serve the major objective of economic planning and economic growth. In the scheme of devolution of the Planning Commission also the underdeveloped States received less than the developed ones. For instance, the per capita assistance for Bihar was Rs. 5.00 in the First Plan, Rs. 18.75 in the Second Plan, Rs. 43.60 in the Third Plan Rs. 57.00 in the Fourth Plan and Rs. 37.00 in the Fifth Plan as against the per capita Central assistance for all States Rs. 24, Rs. 26, Rs. 55, Rs. 99 and Rs. 57.81 in the First, Second, Third, Fourth and Fifth Plan respectively. In a recent study, the National Institute of Public Finance and Policy has shown that "some of the poorer states like Bihar, Madhya Pradesh and Uttar Pradesh have got substantially lower per capita transfers than the all States average both during the annual plan and the Fourth Plan Periods."

The Seventh Finance Commission of India has tilted the balance in favour of Poor States. It has classified that States into six groups (A to F) according to per capita income, the poorer getting more capita devolution than the richer ones. In Bihar we have received the recommendations with mixed feeling. Bihar is one of the poorest States of India and yet it has been refused grants under Article 275 of the Constitution by reducing the estimated deficit of Rs. 3552.14 crores to

Rs. 1057.53 crore. Thereby the State is made to have a surplus of Rs. 1057.53 crore in the revenue account and hence refused grants. However, the State has been given grants of Rs. 63.02 crore for the upgradations of basic administrative infrastructure. The States will also be benefited by Rs. 182.65 crore in the capital account on account of debt-relief recommended by the Commission.

In general the total devolution to Bihar is of the order of Rs. 2212.87 crore which is 10.62 per cent of the total devolution for the country as a whole. Under the award of the Sixth Finance Commission, Bihar got devolution of Rs. 844.72 crore constituting 8.79 per cent of the total devolution. Thus in comparison to Sixth Finance Commission, the devolution to Bihar under the award of the Seventh Finance Commission has increased by 161.96 per cent. The per capita transfer to Bihar is Rs. 393, next to Orissa having a per capita transfer of Rs. 449. But still Bihar may be considered as a loser. First, the overall transfer to Bihar is only Rs. 1155.30 crore, i.e. Rs. 205 per capita as against Rs. 3004.73 crore surplus, i.e. 596 per capita for Maharashtra. The three richest States of India, viz., Punjab, Haryana, Maharashtra are having the highest per capita surplus of Rs. 597, Rs. 676 and Rs. 596 respectively. This disparity in surplus is a cause of concern and therefore some members of the Commission pleaded for surplus equalization approach. Secondly, Bihar is loser in the sense that under Raj Krishna allocation, the State would have secured a total devolution of Rs. 3143.54 crore, i.e. Rs. 558 per capita, which was the highest. Thirdly, the Commission has over-estimated the additional resource mobilization of Rs. 67.33 crore during the period for Bihar and on the other hand reduced the deficit of the State by about Rs. 25.00 crore, which has prevented Bihar from qualifying for grants under Article 275 of the Constitution.

The main departure in the scheme of devolution formulated by the Seventh Finance Commission lies in the allocation of the divisible pool of Central excise. According to the Commission the shares of the States in the divisible pool of excise has been of the per capita state domestic product, the percentage of the poor in each State and a formula of revenue equalization. Each of these principles has been given equal weight of 25 per cent to determine the shares of the States in the divisible pool. The aforesaid multiple criteria, no doubt, tilted the balance in favour of poor States. But its redistributive impact has been to a great extent neutralized by the principle governing the distribution of Income-tax. Like the Second, Fifth and Sixth Finance Commission, the Seventh Finance Commission has decided that 90 per cent of the net proceeds of income tax shareable with the States should be distributed among them in the population ratio and 10 per cent of the divisible pool of income tax should be distributed among States in the same proportion of their contribution to income tax revenue. The adoption of such conflicting double criteria in the distribution of income tax and central excise duty is self-contradictory because the redistributive fiscal impact accelerated by the operation of the formula of the Central Excise duty is contradicted by the principle of devolution of income tax oriented in favour of richer States. The result being that whereas the average per capita income of highest spectrum State is more than twice that of the lowest spectrum State, the difference in average per capita transfer as evolved by the Seventh Finance Commission for the highest spectrum State and the lowest spectrum State is of Rs. 56 only, i.e. about 16 per cent. Thus the difference in per capita transfer of the richest and poorest State is not progressively graduated and less than commensurate to the differences in per capita income and, therefore, the redistributive impact generated by the scheme of devolution is too feeble to mitigate the extent of acute regional economic disparity caused by the previous Sixth Finance Commission in favour of richer States by higher transfer which has been such as to involve a long time lag for the poorer States to come on the equal footing.

This leads us to extend our support to the Raj Krishna Scheme of devolution as suggested by him in his scientific note of incorporated in the report of the Seventh Finance Commission. We have been pleading convincingly that the criterion of collection is not progressive, that origin of income cannot be determined and the contribution criterion is inequitable and therefore time is ripe for the Finance Commission to discard the criterion of collection, lock, stock and barrel. Almost all the Finance Commissions have been feeling uneasy about this criterion but could not be bold enough to reject it and the same applies with the Seventh Finance Commission. But Mr. Raj Krishna in his note of dissent has contended that no weight should be attached to collection in the devolution of income tax revenue and the same formula of inter-state allocation be applied to the devolution of the shareable excise as well as income tax revenues. The formula suggested by Raj Krishna is:

(Population) × (Poverty Ratio) × (Inverse of per capita income)

This formula yields a more progressive allocation and ensures both vertical justice and horizontal justice and contemplates larger resource transfer to the most poverty-stricken States; hill States and especially handicapped States. Under this scheme eight States with a large share of India's poverty and population viz; West Bengal, Bihar, Orissa in Eastern India, Kerala and Tamil Nadu in Southern India, Uttar Pradesh and Madhya Pradesh in Central India and Rajasthan in Western India get an extra total allocation of Rs. 2013 crore than under the majority scheme. Eight hill States, viz. Assam, Himachal Pradesh, Jammu and Kashmir, Manipur, Meghalaya, Nagaland, Sikkim and Tripura also get an extra transfer of Rs. 113 crore.

## (III) FINANCE COMMISSION AND PLANNING COMMISSION

In the maintenance of a fair and judicious balance between the respective shares of the Centre and the State Governments, the Finance Commission has had a unique role to play. Among the countries with federal constitutions there is no parallel to the Indian Finance Commission, entrusted with a unique function. This is 'the role of a wise man, a judge between the conflicting claims of the States on the one hand and the Centre on the other'.

In the beginning, even up to the mid-1960's and the Fourth Finance Commission of 1964, this role of the Finance Commission was fairly observed in actual practice. It is only thereafter that the effectiveness of the Commission has been in a way diluted. This is because the Planning Commission, a limb of the Central Government, has increasingly usurped the role of the Finance Commission in deciding national and regional plans and *inter se* financial allocations.

There has in effect been considerable dilution in the Finance Commission. It would appear that the Planning Commission and the Ministry of Finance of the Union Government are very frequently treading on its corns, and have lastly been taking liberties with is recommendations. This normally is done on the plea that Finance Commissions were 'recommendatory and not legislative bodies and that the Government was not obliged to follow their recommendations in entirety'. The situation becomes more anomalous under the extensive use of the system of 'discretionary grants' under Article 282; discretion can very often be the other name of discrimination, between the Centre and the States, and between one State (Gujarat or Rajasthan) and another (West Bengal or Andhra Pradesh).

Upto mid-1989, as many as nine Finance Commissions have submitted their reports. The Commission was set-up in 1951, 1960, 1964, 1968, 1972, 1976 and 1982 Ninth Finance Commission's report was submitted in 1989.

### The Duration of Finance Commission and the Presidents

In India, under Article 280 of the Constitution the President of India is required to appoint a Finance Commission consisting of a Chairman and four members within two years of the commencement of the Constitution and then after every five years or earlier. To quote Chanda, "the provision of a Finance Commission is intended to assure

| *Finance Commission* | *Duration* | *President* |
|---|---|---|
| First | 1952-53 to 1956-57 | K.C. Niogi |
| Second | 1957-58 to 1961-62 | K. Santhanam |
| Third | 1962-63 to 1965-66 | A.K. Chanda |
| Fourth | 1966-67 to 1968-69 | P.V. Rajmannar |
| Fifth | 1969-70 to 1973-74 | Mahavir Tyagi |
| Sixth | 1973-74 to 1978-79 | K. Brahmananda Reddy |
| Seventh | 1979-80 to 1983-84 | J.M. Shetal |
| Eighth | 1984-85 to 1988-89 | Y.B. Chavan |
| Ninth | 1989-90 to 1994-95 | N.K.P. Salve |
| Tenth | 1995-96 to 1999-2000 | K.C. Pant |

the States that the scheme of distribution will not be made by the Union arbitrarily but will be based on recommendations of an independent Commission which will assess the changing needs of the State in making them. It is "to obviate the frequent political pressures to which the Parliament and the Cabinet are likely to be subjected in revising the system of Union-State transfers, that the Indian Constitution provides for the appointment of a Finance Commission whose recommendations must be taken into account in deciding the grants-in-aid of the States' revenues, the sharing of taxes and other matters referred to it". Shri Chanda has further stated: "The Finance Commission is expected to play the role of a wise man, a judge between the conflicting claims of the State, on the one hand, and the centre on the other". The Finance Commission which is main departure in the financial provisions of the Constitution from the scheme of the Government of India Act, 1935, is "an innovation of far reaching importance to the working of the Indian Federal system". Mr. B.N. Rau described the Finance Commission as "a quasi-arbitral body whose function is to do justice between the centre and the states". The Chairman of the Drafting Committee, B.R. Ambedkar visualized the Commission's role in almost exactly the same terms, viz. "to do justice between province and province between the centre and the provinces". T.T. Krishnamachari also declared that the purpose behind the creation of the Finance Commission was "to assure the States that they will have a fair deal".

The Finance Commission has the status and powers of a civil Court. It is an advisory body and the President is not bound to accept its recommendations. As Ananta Shyanam Ayyangar put it in the Constituent Assembly; "the Finance Commission's recommendations are only recommendatory and not obligatory". However, H.N. Kunzru expressed the hope "that a convention will grow up that the government should normally, that is, except in emergencies, accept the recommendations of the Commission". Sir Ivor Jennings opined thus: "These matters are not decided by Commissions.....the problem is almost invariably one of vote Commissions propose but politicians dispose and politicians depend on votes". In practice, the Government of India has treated the recommendations of the Finance Commissions with great respect. Of the various recommendations made by the Finance Commission only two could not be accepted.

The Indian Finance Commission is a unique institution in the world. No other federal Constitution offers an exact parallel to it. The only close analogy is the Commonwealth Grants Commission of Australia. The two bodies, though resembling very much, differ substantially. The Indian Commission is an *ad-hoc* body appointed at an interval of five years or less, while the Australian Commission is a standing body set-up for recommending every year the quantum of federal grants to meet the needs of the claimant States. Unlike the Australian analogue, the Indian Finance Commission has powers to recommend the basis or principles for determining the quantum of shared taxes and their distribution among the States. Again, while the Australian Commission makes recommendations only with respect to federal grants to meet the fiscal needs of the claimant states, the Indian commission, in addition to the fiscal need grants, also recommends specific purpose grants. Thus, the scope and powers of the Indian Commission are wider than those of its Australia counterparts. Thus, the First Finance Commission recommended grants for the promotion of primary education to some States. In the same way, the Third Finance Commission recommended that a sum of Rs. 36 crore be distributed among the States for improvement of communications. The difference between the two Commissions is also apparent from the fact that while in 1954-55, the Australian Grants Commission controlled less than 6 per cent of the federal state transfer, the Indian Commission deals with 25 per cent of such transfers. A larger part of central assistance to the States' grants and loans is disbursed to them in a discretionary manner, and a substantial part of this non-statutory assistance is allocated to the States on the recommendation of the Planning Commission. Discretionary transfer made by the Centre to the State mostly on the recommendation of the planning commission constitutes more than two-thirds of the total transfers from the centre to the States. In other words, it is the Planning Commission, rather than the Finance Commission, that played a key-role in allocation of resources to the States. Thus, successive Finance Commission found them redundant in the face of the Planning Commission.

*Tenth Finance Commission*

The President of India constituted the Tenth Finance Commission with former Defense Minister K.C. Pant as its head on 15th June 1992.

The Tenth Finance Commission would be coterminous with the Eighth Five Year Plan to evolve a formula for the devolution of resources to the States.

Other members of the Finance Commission are: Dr. Debi Prasad Pal, Mr. B.P.R. Vithal, Planning Commission member C. Rangarajan and former Haryana Chief Secretary M.C. Gupta (member-secretary).

The Commission shall make recommendations relating to the following matters:

(a) The distribution between the Union and the States of the net proceeds of taxes which are to be, or may be divided between them under Chapter 1 if Part xii of the Constitution and the allocation between the States of the respective shares of such proceeds; and
(b) The principles which should govern the grants-in-aid of the revenues of the States out of the Consolidated Fund of India and the sums to be paid to the States which are in need of assistance by way of grants-in-aid of their revenues under Article 275 of the Constitution for purposes other those specified in the provision to clause (i) of that article.

In making its recommendations, the Commission shall have regard, among other consideration, to:

(i) The objective of not only balancing receipts and expenditure on revenue account of both the States and Central Government, but also generating surplus for capital investment and reducing fiscal deficit;
(ii) The resources of the Central Government and the demands thereon, in particular, on account of expenditure on civil administration, defense and border security, debt servicing and other committed expenditures or liabilities;
(iii) The maintenance and upkeep of capital assets and maintenance expenditure on plan schemes to be completed by March 31st, 1995 and the norms on the basis of which specified amounts are recommended for the maintenance of the capital assets and the manner of monitoring such expenditure;

(iv) The requirement of States for modernization of administration, such as computerization of land records and providing faster channels of communication up to and above district level and for upgrading the standards in non-developmental sector and the manner in which such expenditure can be monitored;

(v) The revenue resources of the States for the five years commencing on April 1st, 1995, on the basis of the levels of taxation likely to be reached in 1993-94, targets set for additional resource mobilization for the Plan and the potential for raising additional taxes;

(vi) The requirement of the States for meeting the Non-Plan revenue expenditure also keeping in view the potential for raising additional taxes;

(vii) The tax efforts made by the States.

(viii) The need for ensuring reasonable returns for investment by the States in irrigation and power projects, state transport and departmental commercial undertakings and public sector enterprises, etc.; and

(ix) The scope for better fiscal management consistent with efficiency and economy in expenditure.

The Commission may suggest changes, if any, to be made in the principles governing the distribution of:

(a) The net proceeds in any financial year of the additional excise duties leviable under the Additional Duties of Excise (Goods of Special Importance) Act, 1957 in replacement of the sales tax levied formerly by the state governments; and

(b) The grants to be made available to the States in lieu of the tax under the repealed Railway Passengers' Fares Act, 1957.

In making its recommendations on the various matters aforesaid, the Commission shall adopt the population figures of 1971 in all cases where population is regarded as a factor for determination of devolution of taxes and duties and grants-in-aid.

The Commission shall make its report available by the 30th November 1993, on each of the matters aforesaid, covering a period of five years commencing on the 1st April, 1995. The Commission shall indicate the basis on which it has arrived at its findings and make available the State-wise estimates of receipts and expenditure.

The Commission may review the present scheme of Calamity Relief Fund and may make appropriate recommendation thereon.

The Commission may make an assessment of the debt position of States as on 31st March, 1994 and suggest such corrective measures as are deemed necessary also keeping in view the financial requirements of the centre.

## Comparison of Ninth and Tenth Finance Commission

The following Comparison can be taken into consideration:

The terms of reference of the Ninth Finance Commission created a lot of controversy on several counts. First a binding guideline was given to the Commission for using a normative approach to estimate the revenue receipts and expenditures of the state governments. Second, the Word "Shall" was used in indicating the guidelines to the terms of reference. This word was found to be inconsistence with the fiscal autonomy of the states. Third, there was also reference to examining the possibility of merging additional union excise duties with the basic excise duties and distributing a portion of the total yield from a single divisible pool of union excise duties.

The terms of reference of the Tenth Finance Commission are bound to become controversial in spite of the fact the word "shall" does not appear in the guidelines. This time the controversial part of the terms of reference is "the objective of not only balancing the receipts and expenditure on revenue account of both the states and central government but also generating surplus for capital investment and reducing fiscal deficit. Another controversial aspect is the extension of the scope of Finance Commission's scrutiny from the earlier three public undertakings of the state governments, namely, irrigation project, electricity boards and State Transport undertakings.

## The Problem of Co-ordination Between Finance Commission and Planning Commission in India

National economic planning in India has resulted in considerable centralization of resources. The Planning Commission has emerged as an important agency for central transfers along with the Finance Commission. There is an overlap of functions and duality of authority and both the Finance and Planning Commissions carry out independent revenue exercises for estimating each State's position on non-plan account. On the whole, the Finance Commission's role has been considerably restricted by the activities of the Planning Commission. The non-plan grants are normally administered by the Finance Commission while the planning grants are allocated by the Planning Commission. An interesting feature of grants in India is that while the Planning Commission has not been bestowed any statutory status, it controls the determination and allocation of 75 per cent of the total grants. On the other hand, Finance Commission having a constitutional status has a secondary role to play in the allocation of resources transfers. To quote K. Venkataraman, "Article 282 has been over-worked to a point where it has over-shadowed its substantive brother, Article 275."[9]

In the words of D.R Gadgil, "planning has put a significant part of financial arrangement between the Union and the States out of the purview of the Finance Commission." According to him, "the problems of Federal Finance that confront us are in the event, problems arising out of developments that had not been foreseen by the framers of the constitution, and for which consequently, no provisions have been made in that document. The Finance of development planning has created not only a number of new problems but also a duality of authority within this sphere. Duality arises because while the plan covers both the revenue and capital expenditure, the main function of the Finance Commission under the Constitution is to make recommendations regarding the devolution of revenue resources."

The Finance Commission of 1957, which first dealt with these problems, felt: "some anomalies inevitably arise where the functions of the two Commissions, the Finance Commission and the Planning Commission over-lap." The Commission further says, "So long as both these Commissions have to function, there appears to be a real need for effectively coordinating their work". The Third Finance Commission declared that, "the role and functions of the Finance Commission as provided in the Constitution can no longer be realized fully due to the emergence of the Planning Commission as an apparatus for national planning". The Chairman of the Fourth Finance Commission observed, "After 15 years of the working of provisions of the Constitution, during which period four finance commissions have been appointed, I think the time is ripe to have a review of the Union-State financial relationship particularly in view of the setting up of the Planning Commission". The Fifth Finance Commission started that, "the transfer of funds recommended by the Finance Commission can only partially fulfil the objectives of equalization in view of the division of functions which now exists between the Planning Commission and Finance Commission whereby the former looks after developmental needs and gives plan grants for this purpose". The Sixth Finance Commission also noted, "That the Planning Commission has emerged as an effective instrument for raising the scale of transfer of resources from the Centre to the States", but it felt that it "does not in any way detract from the efficiency of the provisions embodied in the Constitution". The study team of the Administrative Reforms Commission also viewed this problem with anxiety.

Thus, all the Finance Commissions have been feeling uneasy about their relationship with the Planning Commission whose work generally impinges on theirs but whose constitution and methods of work have been very different from theirs. In the context of a virtually monopolistic dominance of a single political party at the Centre and the States, national planning brought about a significant measure of uniformity of policy and administration in the economic field blurring the demarcation of responsibilities laid down in the Constitution. Santhanam goes to the extent of saying that "planning has superseded the federation and our country is working as a unitary system in many respects". It is the view of Tarlok Singh that "national planning widens the scope of the centre and tends to reduce the distinction between Centre and State responsibilities". The Planning Commission has been described as a "New Leviathan" and a "Super Cabinet", though it is not a statutory body but only the creation of the executive.[10]

Planning has seriously upset the financial balance of power established by the Constitution. This has resulted from the increasing resort to discretionary plan grants under Article 282 of the Constitution. This Article was inserted in the constitution as a residuary provision for making financial adjustments between the Union and the States. The Article is intended to give power to the Union and the States to make grants for special bodies and purposes like the United Nations and other International Bodies and to any State in case of a serious natural calamities like famines, floods and earthquakes. For the normal budgetary difficulties of the States, Central grants-in-aid under Article 275 (1) were expected to serve as the main instrument for the necessary devolution of funds. The emergence of planning has entirely changed the expected situation. Article 282 has become the backbone of federal planning finance. It is being extensively used to regulate financial relations between the Union and the States. All Capital grants to the States by the Union for implementing their respective share of the Five Year Plans are now made under this Article as falling within the scope of "public purpose" by the Planning Commission. The Study Team on Financial Relations of the Administrative Reforms Commission held that the administration of plan-grants under Article 282 is constitutional but suggested that the marginal heading against the Article should disappear.

The figures indicate that only one fourth of the total resources transferred from the Centre to States are administered by the finance commission whereas 75% of the transfer is discretionary and distributed by the Planning Commission and the Central Government, sometimes without any rational criteria. Thus, not only the Finance Commission has been superseded but also the financial autonomy of the States has been adversely affected. Politics has also crept in the allotment of Central transfer. This is a situation which needs rectification. These figures also reveal that there is increasing dependence of the States on the centre and, therefore, symptomatic of an unhealthy sign. Commenting on the major role of the discretionary transfer, the Study Team on Financial Administration appointed by the Government of India observes, "It was thus the Planning Commission, rather than the Finance Commission, that began to play the major role in the allocation of resources to States. This was hardly a position contemplated by the constitution".

The pre-dominant role of the Planning Commission with heavy flow of discretionary plan grants has also given rise to many other complications. First, in estimating resources of States both the Commissions make independent exercises which sometimes differ. Secondly, the States' underestimate their resources before the Finance Commission to get more grants and overestimate their resources before the Planning Commission to get more plan grants by demonstrating their matching capacity. Thirdly, the role and working of Finance Commission has been seriously restricted. In the words of the Third Finance Commission, "the role of Finance Commission comes to be, at best, that of an agency to review the forecasts of revenue and expenditure submitted by the States and acceptance of the revenue elements of the plan as indicated by the Planning Commission for determining the quantum of devolution and grants-in-aid to be made; and at worst its function is merely to undertake an arithmetical exercise of devolution, based on amounts of assistance for each State already settled, by the Planning Commission to be made under different heads on the basis of certain principles to be prescribed". Fourthly, the increasing discretionary grants by the Planning Commission have disturbed the balance of Union-State financial relation in favour of the Centre.

The Study Team of Financial Administration adds, "The acceptance of a planned process of development has introduced a new dimension with regard to the Centre-State Relations—a dimension that was not thought of at the time of Constitution-making". The Finance Commission as explained earlier have also expressed their concern for this unusual trend. The Chairman of the Fourth Finance Commission in a separate minute stated that, "it is setting up of the Planning Commission that has in practice restricted the scope and function of the Finance Commission". Mr. Rajamannar declared further that, "the set-up of the Planning Commission inevitably has led to a duplicate and which has resulted in the curtailment of the functions of the Finance Commission". In 1962, T.T. Krishnamachari, the then Union Minister without portfolio suggested, "a re-examination of the relationship between Centre and the States and their respective spheres of power". The Second Finance Commission also felt that the scope of the work of the Finance Commission in assessing the needs of the State has become restricted as a result of the setting up of the Planning Commission".

### Demarcation of the Functions of Planning Commission and Finance Commission

The duality and overlap of functions between the Finance Commission and Planning Commission is not only causing practical difficulties but has also blurred the entire Union and State financial relations in India. Besides the Teams of Administrative Reforms Commission and the Finance Commission, eminent jurists, journalists, politicians and academics like Dr. D.R. Gadgil, K. Santhanam, Tarlok Singh, K.V. Rao, Morris Jones, T.T. Krishnamachari, P.V. Rajamannar, G. Ramchandra, P.R. Dubhasi, M.C. Setalvad, K. Subba Rao, K.M. Panikar, C. Anandurai, Ashok Chand, K. Bombwall, D.T. Lakdawala, K.V.S. Shastri, S.P. Aiyar, P.R. Brahmananda and a host of others have deplored the overlap of functions between the Planning Commission and the Finance Commissions and have suggested remedies which fall under three categories.

In the first place, the Second Finance Commission of India suggested that "so long as both these commission have to function, there appears to be a real need for effectively co-coordinating their work", Mr. D.T. Lakdawala subscribes to the same view when he says that (a) the Finance Commission and the Planning Commission both work together to a common goal in their own spheres with the same tastes in a spirit of non-grudging co-operation or (b) the functions were made absolutely so distinct that each could operate its own criteria within its demarcated boundary without impinging on the utility of the other. But this suggestion of co-ordination and co-operation is not to solve the basic problem. It may facilitate the arithmetical exercises in the distribution of resources but it cannot solve the basic problem of increasing reliance on the discretionary Central grants on the part of States which limits their Financial Autonomy.

The second suggestion has been that the Finance Commission should be altogether abolished and the entire function of the distribution of resources between Centre and States be entrusted to the Planning Commission. This idea emancipated from the report of the Third Finance Commission and received support in certain quarters. The Commission suggested that to remove the anomalous position, either the function of the Finance Commission should be so enlarged as to include the whole financial assistance, non-plan and plan, revenue and capital, to the States or the Planning Commission should be transformed into the Finance Commission at the appropriate time. The former type of arrangement is found in Malaysia where the National Finance Council is concerned with the distribution of taxes and grants and the loan requirements of the federal and State Governments and with certain aspects of economic development and Planning. In India with the existing composition and status of the Planning Commission the idea of entrusting total devolution to the Planning Commission cannot receive the support of States, which have hoarded their faith in the impartiality of the Finance Commissions. It is also not desirable in the interest of federal polity and State autonomy. This is because the Planning Commission is not a statutory body but only a creation of the Central executive. It is chair manned by the Prime Minister and the representation of the Central Ministers also dominates the scene. It is not a judicial or independent body. If, at all, the whole function of resource transfer is entrusted to the Planning Commission it will have to be made a statutory body by amending the Constitution and its composition will have to be completely changed to give it an impartial, non-political and independent complexion. According to one expert, "the acceptance of the second alternative suggestion will, of course, be against the spirit of the federal polity". The study Team on Centre-State Relationships examined this alternative in detail and rejected it. It may, therefore, be concluded that "Planning Commission is hardly the agency to undertake this important function".

The Third suggestion that the entire devolution of resources should be left to the Finance Commission is the only solution to the problem of overlapping and State autonomy. The solution was suggested as the first alternative by the Third Finance Commission. The Commission suggested that "the function of the Finance Commission should be so enlarged as to include the whole financial assistance, non-plan and plan, revenue and capital to the States". At present the total Central assistance that is given to the States falls into four main categories. First, there are the statutory grants under the award of the Finance Commissions; second, there are the plan-grants and loans given to the States on a matching basis. Third, there are the plan grants and loans for schemes which do not call for matching contributions from the State Governments. Fourth, there is the plan assistance largely by way of loans provided for specific identifiable projects of a manufacturing type or infrastructural in character such as irrigation, transport, power generation, water works, etc. all except the statutory grants currently fall within the purview of the Planning Commission. This is peculiar arrangement. The Study Team on Centre-State Financial Relationships, commenting on this arrangement stated, "had the financial provisions of the Constitution been framed at a time when the Planning Commission was in full operation, it is a matter for conjecture whether the determination of the budgetary needs of the States would have been entrusted to two separate bodies viz. the Finance Commission and the Planning Commission". The Team further suggested that "an ideal solution would be to device machinery that would singly have charge of the total problem of plan and non-Plan needs and thus be able to develop well co-ordinate solution to the different aspects of the problem. The machinery should function on a continuous basis. It should operate independently enough to inspire confidence amongst the States and yet not in so detached a way as to be cut off reality".

On the whole, we suggested that all these grants, loans, and the divisible pool of taxes be placed at the disposal of the Finance Commission and that the proportion of discretionary grant should be reduced to a bare minimum necessary of Central authority to make marginal adjustments. It will promote greater initiative on the part of the States and will reduce the possibility of Union-State friction if the allocation of the bulk of the grants is made on the recommendations of the Finance Commission in place of Planning Commission. The disposal of entire devolution of funds by the Finance Commission will make this body more effective, will solve the problem of duality and over-lap of functions, promote concerted calculation and scientific allotment of funds and will safeguard the sentiment and autonomy of the States. It is claimed that such a device would also serve to co-ordinate the various resources of assistance, insure an optimum mobilization of national resources both at the Centre and the State level and enforce better budgetary and financial discipline. At present the Finance Commission has no control over the pattern of expenditure of the devaluated resources. But re-organized Finance Commission will have to make some judgments on the relative efficiency of the expenditure. "The Finance Commission will have to give general guidelines about the attained levels of performance of development in many indicators in the different States".

## NOTES AND REFERENCES

1. R.P. Verma, Federal Financial System in India, 1979, p. 90.
2. B.D. Basu: Introduction to the Constitution of India, 1980, pp. 283-84.
3. S.K. Ray, Indian Economy, Prentice Hall of India (Pvt.) Ltd., 1987, p. 489.
4. *Ibid.*, p. 489.
5. P.K. Jha, Federal Finance in Developing India, Capital Publishing House, Delhi, 1983, p. 119.
6. *Ibid.*, p. 121.
7. Text of Notification by President of India issued on 15th June, 1992.
8. Civil Service Chronicles, September 1992.
9. P.K. Jha, p. 133.
10. *Ibid.*, p. 135.

# Union-State Conflicts

## CENTRE-STATE CONFLICTS ON FINANCES

In the last few years, especially after 1987, there has been growing conflict and tension between the Indian Union and the states in the matter of finance. This conflict has often been aggravated by political and ideological differences between the different parties governing the Centre and the States.

The framers of the Indian Constitution provided for grants and loans so that the Centre might come to the help of those States which were in difficulty and also to bring about balanced development of the different regions. The use of grants and loans in the last 30 years or so, however, has resulted in the complete domination and control of the States by the Centre and to a certain extent, even financial irresponsibility and indiscipline on the part of the States. The enormous increase in transferred resources from the Centre to the States, the phenomenal growth in loan assistance to the states and the political pressure amounting to blackmail by the Centre through the instrument of grants have brightened the States. Hence, there has been an insistent demand for a comprehensive review of Centre-State relations in general and Centre-State financial relations in particular. The J.K. Thavaraj Committee (Report of the Taxation Enquiry Committee, Kerala Government), the Rajamannar Committee on Centre-State relations appointed by the DMK Government of Tamil Nadu and the document on Centre-State relations (1978) adopted by the West Bengal cabinet led by the CPI-M United Front—all these have the same theme viz., political and financial autonomy for the States and drastic restriction of the power and financial resources of the Centre.

**Responsibility and Resources of the Centre and of the States**

According to the Constitution, the Centre has to concern itself with the most generalized features of the Indian economy such as the creation and maintenance of the banking system, railways and ports as well as facilities for national economic planning with the regulation and development of large scale industries, exploitation of mineral resources, regulation of foreign trade, etc., besides, of course, the defense of the nation from foreign aggression. On the other hand, the States are concerned with important aspects of the life of the people, such as the maintenance of law and order, the construction and maintenance of irrigation, power, road transport, etc. the development of educational and health facilities, the promotion of primary sector as agriculture, fisheries, forests and secondary sector viz., tiny, small and medium industries.

In order to carry out these responsibilities the Constitution provided for different types of financial resources. The Union is entrusted with taxes on personal incomes and profits of companies, excise duties and customs duties. In the case of the States, land constitutes an important base of taxation. In a densely populated country like India, the volume of land coming under tax remains almost stationary. Therefore, land, as a source of revenue has been responsible for the inelastic nature of State revenues. Besides, the various taxes on commodities and services (Like sales tax) have not been very productive. On the other hand, taxation of industrial and commercial properties has been the preserve of the Centre, and tremendous expansion in the base of the industrial and commercial property, income and wealth as a result of economic development has been responsible for raising the financial resources of the Centre. At the same time while rapid industrial development boosted excise duty collection, expansion of imports pushed up customs duty collection. This seems to have given buoyancy to the central revenues which is not available to any tax head assigned to the States.

The period since 1951 has witnessed an enormous expansion of financial powers of the Central Government whose dimensions have progressively increased in relation to the combined resources of all State Governments put together. For instance, the current tax revenues of the Centre have risen from Rs. 360 crores in 1950-51 to Rs. 31,900 crores in 1987-88. On the other hand, current tax revenues of the States (excluding transfers from the Centre) have risen from Rs. 280 crores in 1951-52 to Rs. 19470 crores in 1987-88. While the rate of growth of revenues of the Centre is by 88 times, that of the states was only by 70 times. But then, the Centre has limited functions to perform while the functions of the States are almost unlimited.

In a way, the Constitution itself is responsible for the existence of a financially strong Centre and weak States. Until partition, there was a growing consensus in favour of the corporation tax and export duties to be included in the divisible pool. This was the case made out before the Sircar Committee known as the Expert Committee on Financial Provisions. It was partition which alerted the Constituent Assembly against possible dangers to the unity of India arising from the divisive forces. Its effect is reflected in the strong Centre theme which runs through the Constitution clearly reflect this strong Centre bias.

## Sources of Conflict Listed by the States

West Bengal, Jammu and Kashmir, Punjab, Maharashtra and other Southern States are very agitated over the question of state's autonomy. The Centre-State conflict on financial relations is only a part of the overall Centre-State relations and the demand for political and fiscal autonomy. The sources of conflict as listed by the states are as follows:

(i) The basic assumption of the Constitution in favour of a strong Centre and weak dependent states in no longer acceptable and States like, West Bengal insist that a strong Centre requires equally strong and autonomous States.

(ii) The nature of functions to be performed by the State and the necessity to promote cultural, linguistic and the special conditions of each State require that States should be autonomous.

(iii) Since Independence, the Centre has been gradually extending its functions in such a way as to keep the States completely dependent on it. This process has been encouraged in the first two decades after Independence by the Congress Party which was in power both, at the Centre, and at the States. The process was further strengthened during the period of Emergency, 1975-77.

(iv) The Centre has been duplicating unnecessarily a number of departments which have no real functions to perform, i.e., education, public health, etc. which are all State subjects. There is even a move that these subjects should be put on the concurrent list.

(v) The Centre has been interfering in the affairs of the State even in the field of law and order which is purely a State subject by setting up the Central Reserve Police, the Border Security Force, the Industrial Security Force, etc.

(vi) The Centre, with too little to do, is entrusted with too much financial resources while the State Government with so many vital functions to perform is starved of financial resources.

(vii) The financial resources of the Centre are highly elastic, while those of the States are relatively inelastic. Accordingly, the States have been forced to depend upon the Centre to a large extent for their financial requirements.

## States Complaint on Financial Arrangements

As the share of taxes and duties was inadequate to meet the growing revenue and capital expenditure (especially before the Seventh Plan award) the States had to resort more and more to grants-in-aid and loans from the centre. There was a growing feeling of uncertainty and indecision, loss of initiative and irritation on the part of the States. The States have become further suspicious of the behavior and motives of the Centre on the question of raising and sharing of tax revenues with the States.

(a) The Centre has not taken sufficient initiative to impose all the taxes under Article 269 whose proceeds would go to the States.

(b) The corporation tax was the States from the scope of sharing with the States from the very beginning. The States feel sore because their contribution to the development of the corporate sector is quite large. For example, they incur considerable expenditure in providing the direct infrastructural facilities like power, water, raw materials, roads, lands, etc. besides they provide considerable financial incentives for the setting up of industries. It is, therefore, fair and appropriate that the States should have a share in the proceeds of the corporation tax as well.

(c) The central excise duties have been expended by including under it a growing number of items previously taxed by the States.

(d) The divisible pool of excise duties has been limited to basic duties and additional excise duties; the special and auxiliary duties have been kept out of the divisible pool. The rates of additional excise duties which have to be shared with the States were kept low, while raising steadily the rates of excise duties and of special and auxiliary duties which are not to be shared with the State or to be shared only in smaller proportions.

(e) The railway passenger tax whose proceeds were to go to the States was abolished and the Centre fixed arbitrarily a grant in lieu of railway passenger tax. This grant is much less than what the railway passenger tax would have brought to the States.

(f) The surcharges on income tax were imposed by the Central Government but the proceeds were not shared with the States. The Central Government raised the exemption limit of income tax gradually of Rs. 18,000 and reduced the divisible pool. The Central Government, however, did not suffer much loss, as the loss was more than offset by the increase in the surcharge.

(g) The main source of revenue of the States is the sales tax which accounts for 60 per cent of the States' own tax revenue. The Centre wants to abolish the sales tax. There are also proposals to abolish octroi duties and state excises. Again, the Planning Commission had asked the states to raise resources by enhancing electricity charges. But in the 1978-79 budgets, the Centre decided to tap this source also by imposing excise duties on electricity, thus removing the scope for raising electricity tariff by the States (this was given up later). The States are thus left with no proper resources to raise their revenues by depending upon the Centre. The States are running the risk of losing their economic independence.

While the revenues of the States are increasing only gradually, the expenses of the States are increasing at a fast rate. For instance, state plan outlays are increasing with every five year plan. Besides, the various policies of the Central Government (monetary, fiscal and general economic policies) affect the price situation in the country. Whenever there is a rise in price level, there is naturally a demand for increased D.A. from the government and semi-government employees. As the Central Government has vast financial resources to meet such demands, it has no problem; but the State Governments find it difficult to meet such periodical demands from their staff. It is important, therefore, that the Centre consults the States before agreeing to the grant of additional D.A. and provides resources to the States for this purpose.

Too much dependence of the States on the Centre in the form of grants-in-aid and loans has had four serious adverse consequences. Firstly, the Centre could be generous or mean to the different States. Some of the States have felt it humiliating to make frequent visits to New Delhi for funds. A second difficulty is the uncertainty in the budgeting of the States. For instance, in the absence of firm commitments of the Central Government in the matter of grants-in-aid, it is difficult for the States to decide about the various projects of development they have to undertake. A third difficulty is that the States are not able to fulfil the various electoral promises because of inadequacy of financial resources. Finally, most States have resorted to unauthorized overdrafts to finance plan projects.

## Regional Imbalances as a Source of Conflict

A serious complaint of some of the States like Kerala is about the regional imbalance in industrial development. The complaint is that the Centre has not used its fiscal dominance over States to correct regional imbalances. Nor has the Centre used other instruments as its disposal to narrow down the unevenness in regional development. In the absence of integrated approach to the development of the backward regions, location of the Central sector projects and even the location of private industries through licensing policy have not created much of an impression on the problem of regional imbalances. In fact, regional disparities have worsened during the plans. When the Planning Commission was set-up, it was thought that it would bring about a closer economic integration of the country through rapid increase in national income, higher standards of living of the masses, reduction of inequalities between regions, expansion of agriculture, industry, power and transport. While some degrees of economic development has been achieved in every direction. Yet from the point of view of balanced regional development, may be said to be a dismal failure.

Now, with the acceleration of the planning process the responsibilities and commitments of States have increased much more than their financial resources. The result was a kind of centralization at the federal level bringing the economic functioning of the State Governments under Central directive and control through the mechanism of grants and loans. Correspondingly, the financial powers of the States are far too meager in relation to their clearly defined responsibilities. It was really unfortunate that the framers of the Indian Constitution could not visualize the financial implications of large-scale programs of planned development.

## The States' Demand

The Rajamnnar Committee on Centre-State relations (it submitted its report in May 1971) and the West Bengal Memorandum have come out with a string of suggestions and recommendations aiming at autonomy of the states, consistent with the integrity of the country. The suggestions of the West Bengal Memorandum, which have revived the controversy on the question, are as follows:

(a) The powers and functions of the Centre and the State should be clearly marked and specified, and if necessary, TE Constitution should be amended suitably.

(b) The Centre's Jurisdiction should be restricted to defense, foreign affairs and foreign trade, communications, currency and economic co-ordination. All other powers should be exclusively reserved for the States. There should be no interference or control by the Centre in the exercise of its powers by the States.

(c) The present instrument of Centre's control and interference in the affairs of the States viz., the Indian Administrative and Police Services, the Central Reserve Police, the Border Security Force, the Industrial Security Force, etc. should be removed forthwith.

(d) The Planning Commission and the National Development Council which have an important role in planning and economic co-ordination should be specifically referred to in the Constitution.

(e) 75 per cent of the central revenues should be qutomatically transferred by the Centre to the divisible pool of the States and Finance Commission would have power only to recommend the principles for the distribution of this divisible pool among the States.

Other important suggestions made by the West Bengal Memorandum and the Rajamannar Committee on Centre-State relations include equal representation for all States in the Rajya Sabha, the maintenance of the special status of Kashmir in the Indian Union, the retention of English as the link language between the Centre and the States. The right to use mother tongue at all levels, industrial licensing to be vested with the States, except for large companies of national importance, inter-state water disputes to be settled by the Supreme Court, etc.

The problem of Centre-State financial relations is thus a part of the general and more important problem of Centre-State relations. Let us now consider the problem from the angle of the Central Government.

## The Centre's Case

All those who are in favour of a strong Centre, reject the case of States for more functions and for more financial resources. The West Bengal Memorandum would allow the Centre to perform only three or four functions and leave the rest of the functions to the States. The States would like to have a say, at least indirectly, even in the limited powers and functions of the Centre. For example, the States would like to influence the location and distribution of defense industries, the use of foreign exchange reserves, allocation for the projects of communication and also monetary and fiscal policies, etc. at the same time, Centre will be left with only 25 per cent of the revenue raised while 75 per cent of the revenue would go to the States automatically. All these things clearly indicate that the ultimate intention is to have strong states and a weak and emaciated Centre.

Danger to national integrity There is also the fear that some of the States ideologically different from other might like to break away from the federation on some pretext or the other. The DMK ideology at one time, the Khalistan movement in Punjab and Assam agitation-all these have separatist tendencies. The commonly used analogies of autonomous states in the U.S.S.R. and the U.S.A. are not really valid so far as India is concerned. It is the presence of common political ideology and supreme central authority which hold together the culturally diverse autonomous states in the U.S.S.R. while in U.S.A. common language, and commonly held social and moral values hold together autonomous States from falling apart. This is not the situation in India. States autonomy can thus be dangerous to the national integrity.

The argument that 'State autonomy' would liberate creative energies at present inhibited by constant central interference and domination and that state autonomy would promote rapid economic growth is highly questionable in the Indian context. It is the Centre's case that except for communist parties who are wedded to an economic ideology; other regional political parties are very parochial in their outlook. Most of them are financed by big business in industry, trade, transport, films, etc. they are corrupt to the core and destinies of these states are controlled by men, among whom some have very close links with smugglers and anti-social elements. These politicians cannot see beyond their noses and want to use state autonomy to further their selfish ends so as to remain in power. In any case .there is no positive correlation between state autonomy and the rapid develop of different States.

In this connection it should be emphasized that the States do already enjoy considerable autonomy. They have exclusive control over such key sectors as agriculture, irrigation and power, administration, social welfare, law and order, etc. But not all States have performed these functions properly in any appreciable degree. The advanced states have continued to march head and the backward states have remained backward.

The States' complaint about inadequate financial resources and their demand for large taxation powers would sound more reasonable if they had fully exploited the resources they command. They are not only reluctant to tax agricultural income but have been abolishing land levies despite the gaping deficits in their budgets. The financial difficulties thus arise in part from their own lack of political courage. Still the Centre has been sympathetic to their pleas for assistance and their share of the divisible pool of Central taxes has progressively increased over the years.

States generally resort to alternative methods for overcoming their budgetary gaps and this was mostly done through grants-in-aid and loans from the Centre before 1967. After 1967, the non-Congress dominated State and even the Congress-controlled States were in a rebellious mood and they resorted to unauthorized overdrafts on the Reserve Bank, which they insisted should be converted into regular loans. In spite of pressure from the Reserve Bank, these overdrafts continued to create inflationary pressure in the economy and constituted serious financial indiscipline.

The inadequacy of financial resources was sought to be made up by the use of Central grants-in-aid. The grants-in-aid were also meant to help backward States to come up to the level of other. Besides grants, the States approach the Centre for loans and advances. The resources transferred from the Centre have accounted for over 40 percent of the total expenditure of the States.

It is thus clear that the States have become increasingly dependent on the Centre for their expenditure. Such dependence is the natural consequence of the enormous command enjoyed by the Centre over relatively larger and expanding revenue resources. The massive indebtedness of the States had led to a kind of creditor-debtor relationship between the Centre and the States breeding a sense of irresponsibility among the borrowing States. In a sense, the position of dependence on the Centre has suited the States well. It has enabled them to avoid taking unpopular tax measures and to attribute their inefficiency and failure to the Centre.

By 1983, the Centre-State relations were almost at a breaking point—with Khalistan demand for a separate Sikh State, and the Southern States forming a regional council, and so on. It was to settle this problem once and for all that the Central Government appointed the Sarkaria Commission, with comprehensive terms of reference covering constitutional, legislative, financial and administrative aspect of Centre-State relations.

## PROBLEMS OF LESS DEVELOPED STATE IN INDIA

Gap between needs and resources of State Governments, the constitution provides for division of financial power in between the Centre and the States. However, the revenue-raising capacity of the States is restricted because of the nature of taxes assigned to them. Since land is limited, the scope of increasing land revenue is also limited.

Similarly taxes on agricultural income, sales and purchase tax, excise duties on intoxicants, taxes on motor vehicles, entertainments, etc. are also comparatively less elastic than the taxes assigned to the Centre. Because of the economic progress registered by the country in the last three decades, the base of income tax, Union excise duties, customs duties and other important Central taxes has expanded considerably. This has given immense powers to the Central government to increase its resources with the passage of time. This structure of financial relation between the Centre and the State governments—less elastic sources of revenue for the State and more elastic sources of revenue for the Centre—Places the States at a distinct disadvantage. While demands on States' resources are increasing rapidly because of the pressure of development services (especially in the field of social welfare), their income has failed to increase correspondingly, accordingly, the dependence of State governments on the Centre has increased considerably over the years. This has made them vulnerable to increasing pressures from the Central government to tow its lines. Where the State government belongs to a different political party, as in the case of West Bengal, these pressures give rise to open conflict seriously jeopardizing the effectiveness of the policy measures introduced by the concerned State government.

## The Question of State Autonomy

This "strong Centre and the weak State" arrangement was introduced intentionally by the framers of the Constitution in a bid to stall the divisive forces operating in the economy. The partition and is after effects created a strong public opinion in favour of such an arrangement. The one-party rule at the Centre and States further cemented this relationship and the role of States became more and more secondary. As pointed out in the 'Document on Centre-State Relations' adopted by the West Bengal government in December 1979 the structure of the Indian Constitution is more unitary than federal. By vesting all residuary power in the Centre and by keeping 47 items in the concurrent list it strengthened the base of Central control and vested the Central governance with practically unlimited powers to interfere in the governance of States. Though law and order is a State subject, the Centre has not hesitated in interfering in this field through the establishment of the Central Reserve Police, the Border Security Force, the Industrial Security Force, Education, which was till recently a State subject, has been transferred to the concurrent list by the 42nd amendment to the Constitution.

All these processes operating in the political field have considerably eroded the independence of States and their political and economic powers. Therefore, quite recently, demands for increase in State autonomy have been raised by various quarters. While no one denies the importance of a strong Centre for preserving the integrity of the nation, it is necessary to give a serious thought to these demands. Grant of a certain amount of autonomy (at least in the spheres originally contemplated by the Constitution) is necessary to fulfil the democratic ambitions of the people. A 'Strong Centre' without 'Strong States' is not conceivable.

### Reduced Importance of Finance Commission

We have noted earlier that transfers through the Finance Commission (which is a statutory body) contribute only about one-third of total transfers from the Centre to the State. This means that about two-thirds of the transfers are channeled through the Planning Commission or the Central Government directly. For a considerable period of planning, the Planning Commission was not guided by any objective criteria to determine the share of different States in its assistance and this introduced an aura of arbitrariness in the whole transfer mechanism. Since the Centre contributed a large amount of resources in the form of discretionary grants to the States, it acquired considerable powers to affect the decision-making processes at the State level. This led to a further erosion of State autonomy.

### Failure to Tackle the Problem of Regional Imbalance to any Satisfactory Extent

The process of resource transfers through the Planning Commission and the Finance Commission has failed in achieving the avowed objective of reducing disparities. We have already noted that plan assistance is provided 70 percent in the form of loans and 30 percent in the form of grants. Since the ratio is a fixed one and does not discriminate between advanced and backward States, it amounts to discrimination against backward States. Since advanced States have a relatively better economic position they should be granted greater percentage o resources in the form of loans while backward States should receive a larger percentage of grants. Non-compliance to this common sense logic has resulted in a paradoxical situation where the comparatively richer States received a higher per capita grant than poorer States. For example, during 1969-70, rich States like Punjab and Haryana received a higher per capita grant than the poor States like Uttar Pradesh, Madhya Pradesh, Bihar and Andhra Pradesh. Bihar with Lowest per capita income range also received the lowest per capita grant.

As far as transfers through Finance Commission are concerned, all Finance Commissions sought to give due importance to backward States. However, there was no clear-cut bias in favour of backward States.

The ultimate result was that advanced States cornered a major share of the actual devolution of resources from the Centre to the States. For example the four advanced industrial States of Maharashtra, Gujarat, Tamil Nadu and West Bengal have consistently obtained more than one-third of total income tax transfers. However, the distribution of proceeds from Union excise duties was more judicious.

All Finance Commission gave undue importance to budgetary needs while deciding the allocation of grants-in-aid. They did not realize that advanced States could also incur large budgetary deficits,9even deliberately at times) and qualify for larger grants-in-aid. This led to a paradoxical situation in some instances are richer States got more grants-in-aid as compared to poorer States.

The third constituent of resource transfer, viz., discretionary grants is not guided by any distinct philosophy of helping the poorer States to a greater extent. It is guided more by political considerations than by anything else. In any case, discretionary grants also do not seem to have helped the backward States more *vis-à-vis* the advanced States.

## SARKARIA COMMISSION

Government of India, Ministry of Home Affairs vides their notification No. IV/11017/1/83 appointed a Commission under the Chairmanship of R.S. Sarkaria, a retired Judge of Supreme Court "for a fresh comprehensive review of the arrangements between the Union and the States, in all respect". The late Prime Minister Mrs. Indira Gandhi declared in Parliament on March 24, 1983 "the commission will review the existing arrangements between the Centre and the States while keeping in view the social and economic developments that have taken place over the years. The review will take into account the importance of unity and integrity of the country for promoting the welfare of the people".

The Commission submitted its report on October 27, 1987 in two parts, first contains main report while second contains the memoranda received from the State Governments and political parties.

The appointment of Sarkaria Commission was indirectly an acknowledgement of the universally felt need to take a fresh look at the Centre-State relations. We will first deal with the main contention of states and feelings of the Union Government. The recommendations of the Sarkaria Commission and its evaluation will be discussed.

### View Point of the States

Mainly three board groups of suggestions have been put forth by the States to enlarge States' power of taxation, stamp duties and duties of excise on medicinal and toilet preparations levied by the Union and collected as well as appropriated by the States should be transferred to

State List. These goods do not form part of inter-state trade to any large extent. When a tax is administered and collected by the same authority which has the power to appropriate it, general efficiency in taxing is highest.

There are eight entries in Article 269, important being Estate duty as Succession duties on non-agricultural property, terminal taxes on goods and services carried by rail, sea or air, taxes on sale or purchase of newspapers and advertisements therein, etc. which are levied and collected by the Union but assigned to the States. It has been felt by the States that given the freedom, they will be able to garner more resources by levying these taxes. Taxes on lotteries, banking, excise duties on items like sugar, molasses and khandsari and some other items which have been suggested by the State for inclusion in the realm of State's taxation. Besides, the proposal to levy agricultural income tax by the Union and revenue being assigned to the States has not been welcome because of the unhappy experience of the scheme of Additional Excise Duties in lieu of States Tax.

The States in general have also put forth suggestions pertaining to enlargement of the divisible pool so that more resources may be earmarked for the States. It has been suggested that the States may be given a share out of the total tax revenues of the Union on the ground that so long as the total quantum of transfers remains the same, it is immaterial whether the share comes out of specified taxes or out of the total tax receipts. This will enlarge the base and insulate the States to a greater extent form the effects of fluctuations of individual sharable taxes and would thus be given a more predictable and assured share. In order to go over the disincentive on part of the Union Government in raising revenues from income tax and Union Excise and absolving the Union of the criticism of manipulating resources out of the divisible pool, it would be advantageous to make the entire receipts of the Union divisible.

It has also been suggested that percentage share of the States should be built into the Constitution and the Finance Commission then, need concern itself only with the division of such resources among the States. The States have demanded inclusion of corporation income tax in the divisible pool, as was the case before 1959. The States have also been raising the issue of bringing the surcharge on Income Tax in the divisible pool. The experience of raising administered prices of items petroleum, steel, cement, etc., by the Union has deprived the States of a fair amount of financial resources. Therefore, the net increase in receipts on account of raised prices must be shared with the States. It has been further suggested that such sharing should be applicable only in cases where the Central Public Sector enterprises are making profits.

The States have criticized the schemes of special bearer bonds and compulsory deposits as measures to circumvent increases in Income Tax or as directly resulting from the inability of the Union Government to administer the same efficiently. Hence, States demand that the receipts of, these two measures should also be shared with then as they have the same tax base as the mandatorily sharable Income Tax. Besides, as they represent savings, they could be shared like the Small Savings Collections.

The pattern of resource devolution has been a complex issue as far as the States are concerned. The federal transfers are affected through Finance Commission, Planning Commission and the Ministry of Finance. It has been maintained that only statutory transfers, i.e., through the Finance Commission, were envisaged by the Constitution whereas, rest of the transfers under Article 282 were intended to be a sort of residuary. Over the years, discretionary transfers have dominated statutory transfers, thereby, distorting the Constitutional scheme, Inter-State equity in transfers has been to some extent, violated and backward States have demanded use of such formulae which would place more resources at their disposal.

The role of Finance Commission in resource transfers has been the crucial issue in Indian federal financial relations. It has been suggested that the functions of the Finance Commission be enlarged to cover plan and other transfers and /or undertake comprehensive annual/ periodical reviews of the financial performance of the Union and the State Governments. The co ordination between the Finance Commission and the Planning Commission should be improved. Suggestions have also been given to make the Finance Commission a permanent or standing body. A well-equipped secretariat has also been suggested for the Finance Commission to carry out studies and maintain operational continuity.

It has suggested by the States that they should have representatives on the Finance Commission. It is their apprehension that the States' case may go by default unless they are represented on the Finance Commission. Some of the less developed and middle income group states have argued that 'gap-filling approach' by the Finance Commission has led to the phenomenon of huge surpluses with some of the more developed States after devolution and slender or zero surpluses with others.

There have been three instances when the recommendations of the Finance Commission were not accepted. The States strongly protested against such attitude because, besides, causing serious hardship to several States as their expectations for higher devolutions were belied, this also adversely affected the prestige of the Finance Commission. In the context of consignment tax, the State have resented non-implementation of the intent of Constitutional amendment even after the elapse of five years.

The States, over the years have also complained against the levying of additional excise duties in lieu of sales tax on textiles, sugar and tobacco since 1956. It has been maintained that the receipts from additional excise duties were much lower than what they would have got if they had imposed sales tax on them. The States have also advocated a tax on advertisements in newspapers, broadcast and telecast. Further, serious dissatisfaction has been expressed by the State with the inadequate grant given in compensation of the repealed Railway Passenger Fare Tax. In particular, the fixed lump sum grant has been presented by the States, whereas railway earnings have increased manifold.

The State Government have raised quite a valid point that periodical upward revisions of pay, dearness allowance, terminal benefits, etc., of the Central Government employees put pressure on States to revise the allowances of their own employees. With limited resources, States, particularly the less developed, find it very difficult to keep the pace of development.

Some States have alleged payment of inadequate royalty on minerals, petroleum, etc., extracted from their territories. These rates are fixed every four years on the basis of a specific amount per ton, States want more frequent rate revision on *ad valorem* basis to neutralize price increases.

With a view to solve the problem of Union-State financial relations, creation of new institutions has been suggested by the States. In particular two categories of institutions have been suggested; (a) a machinery for consultation and discussion on issues of mutual economic interests between the Union and the State, and (b) institutions, with adequate representation of the States, also for specific purposes such as a loan or credit Council and an Expenditure Commission.

Regarding relief for natural calamities, the States have suggested that these should be treated as national obligation. Relief grants must be given expeditiously and should preferably be outside the plan. In a Welfare State, it is necessary that standard of administration must be upgraded continuously so as to cope with the pressure of development and welfare. For this purpose, grants are disbursed by the Union. However, the States feel that the Central-Level Inter-Ministerial Empowered Committee had been laying down conditions which were difficult for the States to follow for upgradations of standard of administration.

Several State Governments have left that the present arrangements for the allocation of community's savings are unsatisfactory, it is complained that the Union Government has been appropriating for itself a lion's share of the capital resources. On the other hand, mounting burden of debt, servicing has led to serious erosion in resources for development. The States want Plan transfers to have larger grant component that the 30 percent now prevailing. A claim of access to larger market loans has also been put forth by the States. In fact, States share in market borrowing shares come down drastically over the years. With regard to small saving collections, the States have demanded that their share in the additional small savings collection should be increased from the present two-thirds share, and that such loans should be treated as loans in perpetuity.

It has been complained by the States that the terms of channeling external assistance for the projects included in their plans are more unfavorable than those on which the Union Government is provided assistance by the external agencies. Full amount of assistance is also not transferred to the States.

Many State Governments feel uneasy about the problem of overdrafts and attributes it to the basic imbalance in the resource allocation. The overdrafts accrue as a result of unforeseen expenditure on natural calamities, payment of D.A. installment; delays in the release of instalments of assistance for Centrally Sponsored Scheme, etc. the States have suggested that ways and Means Limits need to be determined rationally, in relation to the scale of States' budgetary operations and their seasonal variations. The State Governments have also complained of inadequacy of their resources in relation to their responsibilities as the fundamental structural problem which often compels them to resort to overdrafts.

We have briefly discussed the viewpoint of States with regard to transfer of resources from the Centre. In the context of States' position as recipients of transfers, demand for more funds is quite obvious. In a nut shell we can summarize the demand of States as transfer of more tax heads, enlargement of divisible pool, modifications in the working of Finance Commission and other related matters. At this juncture, a balanced view can only emerge after we consider the viewpoint of the Union Government also.

## Viewpoint of the Union

In all the federations of the world, the revenue of the federal Governments have grown enormously during the past half a century, in our country, sources of revenue with the Union are not entirely meant for its exclusive use but are to be shared with the States mandatorily as in the case of Income Tax and optionally, with the approval of the Parliament, in the case of Union Excise Duties. Over the years, the Centre has also complained of widening gap between resources and needs. Its own resources are no more elastic than those or the States. There is need for the States to make greater effort to increase resources within their existing powers, before seeking more powers or large Central assistance. Mere transfer of resources from the Centre can only be a temporary measure at the cost of wider national interests.

In the context of stamp duties under Entry 91 (Listal) the Union Government has maintained that it is desirable to have uniform rates throughout the country in commercial and related transactions. Its transfer to the State List may result in inter-state disparities in their rates and tax regulation which may play havoc with commercial activity and free flow of trade.

The States have not been allowed to levy tax on advertisements in newspapers, radio or television, because papers with an India-wide circulation may face cost differential among States, adversely affecting their circulation and financial viability. Besides, such a tax, if levied will be disadvantageous to the less developed with low urbanization and thin readership because the proceeds of such a tax are to be distributed on the recommendations of the Finance Commission among the States within which it is levied.

In the context of States' demand to levy State Corporation Tax, the Centre argued that such a tax in the Union List ensures uniformity of approach to the taxation of corporate incomes and profits. Such arrangement secures greater efficiency in the administration of this tax. The problems which arise in determining the locale of income accruals where units and offices of the same company or undertaking are located in different States are avoided and make erosion of this tax more difficult.

The Central Government has no intention to assume power of taxing agricultural income, Conceptual difficulties are involved in defining agricultural income because of diversity of the quality and productivity of land. The illiterate farmers will not be able to maintain accounts for taxation purposes and may not be able to follow the rules and regulations prescribed. Even the long-term fiscal policy emphasized that, "Land revenue and taxation of agricultural income are States' subjects under the Constitution." The Centre has no intention of seeking any change in this position.

The Union Ministry of Finance opposed inclusion of corporation Tax in the divisible pool because there is no such provision in the Constitution and the disadvantage to the States due to definitional change in 1959 has been compensated by the Finance Commission by raising States' share or income tax. Besides the Union Government has faced resource crunch after 1959. The very fact of a tax being elastic should not be as a justification for its sharing.

Regarding non-imposition of Consignment Tax even after the lapse of five years, the Union Government has explained that power of exemption from such a tax, if vested in the State Government only, will create numerous problems of inter-state disparities. However, concurrent power of exemption with Central Government along with the States will ensure uniformity of taxation on goods and transactions of all India importance throughout the country and also to avoid any marked fluctuations of the prices of the commodities of national importance and those which are subject to the scheme of administered prices.

The Union Government felt that rationale of amending Entry 55 List II was that the revenue from advertisements by radio/television should be fully available for the development of these services. Besides, a tax on such advertisements might seriously erode accrual of revenue from them.

The Union Ministry of Finance, in the context of financing relief works in the wake of national calamities has pointed out that the demands made by State Government are rising sharply and the ultimate relief found necessary a fraction of this demand. Even with this order of relief, the total burden on the Union has been going up steadily year after year and in 1985-86 it was well over Rs. 1200 crores. It is suspected that there is a connection between the very large demands for relief and increasing deficits emerging in the States' budgets. Persistent irresponsibility in this regard by a state should be taken into account by the Finance and Planning Commission in recommending future assistance.

The views of the Union Government regarding various issues of Centre-State financial relations admit that there is resource crunch before the Union Government and the State must harness all the available resources to them and at the same optimize the resources use. The Union Government has compromised in several instances to provide additional resources to the States. The argument of Union Government carries weight that the States have failed to tax agricultural income. As a result of public expenditure in various infrastructural facilities like irrigation, electrification, etc., agricultural income have grown enormously. Therefore, it is quite justified if the increases in income are brought within the tax net. However, on several other points, the Union Government has not yielded to pressure of the States for more devolution of resources. What is essential at this juncture is that objectivity must be used by the Union Government in dealing with various demands of the States. The recommendations of the Sarkaria Commission in this regard are quite realistic and will go a long way towards maintaining balance in Union-State relations.

Main Recommendations of the Commission are:

1. Under the present circumstances, duties on all the items covered by Article 268 do not appear to be a buoyant source of revenue amenable to frequent revisions. Since basic circumstances do not always remain constant, the Union Government should, in consultation with the State Governments, periodically consider and explore the revision or imposition of these duties. The revenue raised from these duties should be separately specified in the budget and other relevant publications.
2. The monetary limit of Rs. 250 per annum fixed 37 years ago on taxes that can be levied on professions, trade, callings and employments (Entry 60 of List II) should be, in consultation with the States, revised upwards immediately and revised periodically.
3. Taxation of agricultural income is a sensitive matter. Both, the Union and the State Government are not inclined at present for a change in the Constitutional provision in regard to Entry 46 of List II. Nonetheless, in view of its potential, the question of raising resources from this source by forging political consensus and the modalities of levying the tax and collection of proceeds, etc. would require an in depth and comprehensive consideration in the NEDC.
4. By an appropriate amendment of the constitution, the net proceeds Corporation Tax may be made permissibly sharable with the States, if and as Parliament may by law so provide. This would have the advantage of enlarging the base of devolution so that in the revenues of the States there would be greater stability and predictability in future. Further, being an elastic resource, the States would benefit from its growth. Consequent on inclusion of Corporation Tax in the divisible pool, adjustments will have to be carried out by suitably bringing down the share of States in Income Tax and Union Excise Duties.
5. The Surcharge of Income Tax should not be levied by the Union Government except for a specific purpose and for a strictly limited period.
6. The organic linkage in policies and measures adopted by different levels of Government in resource mobilization and expenditure must be duly recognized. This, indeed, is the crux of Union-State financial relations. An expert Committee, with suitable representation from the States,

may be appointed by the Union Government to recommend desirable directions of reforms in taxation and *inter alia*, consider the potential for resource mobilization by the Union and the States. The report of this Committee should be placed before the standing Finance Committee of the NEDC for consideration.

7. Substantial expenditure is incurred by both the Union and the State Government on schemes which have come to be known as populist measures. It will be in the best interests of the Concerned Government to take explicity into account the high opportunity cost of such schemes and to examine whether any important programme of development are compromised due to such diversion of scarce resources.
8. It is necessary that a comprehensive paper on direct, indirect and cross-subsidies, covering both Union and State Government, is prepared by the Planning Commission every year and brought up before NEDC for discussion, since the increasing burden of subsidies has a direct relevance to the availability of resources for the execution of the Plan.
9. The present division of labour which has developed over the years between the Finance Commission and the Planning Commission is that the former advises on the non-plan revenue requirements and non-plan capital gap. In certain sectors, where the problem is clear and the numbers are reasonable sure, the Finance Commission has recommended capital resource devolution also only to a limited extent. The present division of responsibilities between the two bodies, which has come to be evolved with mutual understanding of their comparative advantage in dealing with various matters in their respective spheres, may continue.
10. The Finance Commission Cell/Division proposed to be located in the Planning Commission, should continuously monitor the behavior of States' finances. It should also estimate annually the deviations from the norms evolved by the Finance Commission. The Planning Commission would then able to bring before the NEDC annual reviews indicating, among other things, the deviations from the forecast of Finance Commission and the reasons for the same. This would afford an opportunity to the NEDC to monitor effectively and evolve consensus on the

mobilization of resources and contain the non-developmental expenditure.

11. The Finance Commission Division should, in a co-operation with the States, organize comprehensive studies on trends in growth of public expenditure in the States in the light of findings of the previous Finance Commission. The studies conducted by the Finance Commission Division should be available well in time for the use of the next Finance Commission.
12. There is a need to further strengthen the Finance Commission Division. It would result in much closer co-ordination between the Planning Commission and the Finance Commission if this Division were to work under the general supervision of the Member in-charge of financial resources in the Planning Commission. Such an arrangement will also make available to the Planning Commission date and analysis on various parameters relevant for resources discussion for the Plan and reviewing of the finances of the Union and the States.
13. Finance Commission should draw experts for assisting them in their work from various parts of the country. It would be advantageous if suitable experts are drawn from the States also for staffing the Secretariat of the Finance Commission.
14. The step taken by the Union Government to initiate a process of consultation with the States in finalizing the terms of reference of the Finance Commission is in the right direction. It is desirable that this healthy practice of informal consultation with the States in this matter should continue.
15. Consideration of adequate flow of funds to the backward regions in the States would necessitate creation of expert bodies, like the Finance Commission, at State level also, without such an organization at the State level to effect regional distribution, skewness will persist in large pockets even in advanced states. State Planning and Finance Boards may be set-up at state level to take an objective view of resources to be developed to the districts.
16. The crucial role of administrative/organizational support in the backward areas is a since quanon for making the investment effective in consonance with the accepted policy of reducing regional disparities. It may even be desirable to provide in the special terms of reference of the Finance Commission to make available finances, with effective

monitoring arrangements, to fill up the inter-state gap in administrative capabilities. This vital aspect should continue to receive due consideration of the Finance Commission.

17. It is, indeed, unfortunate that the Eighth Finance Commission's final recommendations were not implemented in 1984-85 which caused serious financial problem in some States. While the Union Government in a technical sense, the expectation is that, as far as possible, these would not be departed from without compelling reasons. It is to hope that in future there would be no occasion for such departure. It is necessary that the time-schedule for the completion of Finance Commission's work is so drawn up that it can reasonably submit its final report 4 to 5 months before the beginning of its period of operation.
18. As much of the information gathered by the Finance Commission, as well as the detailed methodology followed by it, is of public interest, it should be got published, say within six months of the publication of the Report, to enable informed discussion and responsible research in the relevant spheres and better appreciation by the State Governments.
19. It is a matter of serious concern that even after a lapse of about five years no legislation has been brought in for giving effect to the intent of the Constitutional amendment enabling levying of the consignment Tax. The Union Government should bring in suitable legislation in this regard without further loss of time.
20. There are complaints that the yields from certain cases levied along with Union Excise Duties under special Acts of Parliament have remained outside the divisible pool of resources. While it may be become necessary for the Union Government to levy such cases in view of Special needs, their application should be for limited duration and for specific purposes only.
21. The scope for raising additional resources to any considerable extent on items covered by Article 269 appears to be limited. An Expert Committee should be constituted to enquire into and review from time to time, in consultation with the States, the operational feasibility of the scope for levying taxes and duties included in Article 269 and the complementary measures the State Government would be required to take.

22. The Constitution should be suitably amended to add the subject of taxation of advertisement, broadcast by radio or television to the present Entry 92 list 1 and Article 269 (1) (f).
23. The Union Government should signify its acceptance of the Finance Commission's recommendation in regard to the grant in lieu of the Railway Passenger Fare Tax also, along with other items, while placing the Explanatory Memorandum before Parliament.
24. The Finance Commission take into account the expenditure liability of the States with respect to dearness allowance, etc., and make a provision for the same. But inflation increases both outlays and revenues. The permanent secretariat of the Finance Commission should make an annual review of the situation. If in any year the net burden of the States seems unduly heavy, the Planning Commission and the Union Ministry of Finance should jointly evolve appropriate relief measures.
25. The review of royalty rates on minerals, petroleum and natural gas should be made every two years and well in time, as and when they fell due.
26. A sub-Committee of Finance of the Standing Committee of the NEDC may be constituted consisting of Union Finance Secretary and the Finance Secretaries of various States and Union Territories. It will consider all such matters calling for co-ordination of economic policies as may be entrusted to it by the NEDC or its standing Committee. This body will report to the standing Committee of the NEDC, Since the Planning Commission would be providing the secretariat support to the NEDC, the same may be extended for this body also. This will ensure expert consideration of various aspects of the problems and adequate consideration of the view of the Union and the States/Union Territories. The role of this Committee will be deliberative and advisory and helpful in forging a consensus of financial matters.
27. The distinction made by the Seventh and Eighth Finance Commission in providing a more favourable flow of Central assistance for floods, cyclones, etc. *vis-a-vis*, a drought situation may continue.
28. The Central Team to assess the damage caused by natural calamities should invariably be headed by the Advisor in charge of that State in the Planning Commission, as was the practice in the past.

In the event of a natural calamity, relief must be given immediately. A procedure which enables States to expeditiously provide necessary succor and relief to the affected people should be evolved in consultation with the States, along with suitable norms in regard to the scale of relief. Formulation of standard formats for submission of memoranda by the States will greatly help the Union in dealing with requests of various States urgently and on a uniform basis.

29. In a calamitous situation, the States should have a reasonable discretion to make inter-district or inter-sectoral adjustments. To allay the apprehension that the expenditure pattern adopted under the stress of urgency may not find approval, norms in regard to items of expenditure which are to be incurred immediately, e.g., relief by way of issue of food grains, clothing and re-building of shelters in the event of floods, may be evolved by the Union and communicated to all State Governments.

    Relief assistance should extend beyond the financial year. The assistance required till next June/July should be decided in the beginning itself so that relief works can be properly planned and executed.

30. There appears to be a tendency to bring in non-productive schemes and programs under the capital head in order to expand the plan size. In future plans, for reasons of financial propriety this sector, through small, has to be weeded out of the capital-budget and put under the revenue budget. It is better to tackle the situation at this stage whilst the problem is marginal.

31. The rationality of transfers from the Union to the States would involve more of revenue transfers to the less developed States with lower repayment capacity and weak financial base. In contrast, keeping in view the needs of development in the advanced States, a suitable mix of budgetary and non-budgetary access to capital resources may be allowed to them. The logic is that such States are in a better position to service commercial borrowings.

32. The flow of capital fund from various sources to the States and their allocation among them should from part of an integrated plan. This task may be attended to by the Planning Commission in consultation with the Ministry of Finance and the Reserve Bank of India and got approved by the NEDC as part of Plan financing.

33. The Union Government should give its consent freely to States for borrowing from borrowing from banks and financial institutions for periods less than one year under Clause (4) of Article 293.

    The Union Government has now allowed the States' public sector units to raise funds 'on merit' by floating bonds. In practice, the considerations relating 'merit' of a States' enterprise should not put them to any disadvantage *vis-a-vis* the Union Government's undertakings.

    The system of tax-free municipal bonds should be introduced in this country.

34. Treatment of small savings loan is a matter of Judgment by the Finance Commission in relation to the overall debt burden of the States. As long as small savings keep increasing and there is a surplus every year after repayment of due loans, the Union is not called upon to repay any loan not already covered by the net transfer principle. If and when the position changes in any year, when the outgo is greater than the inflow, the State would be responsible for their share of the net small savings collections. If a formula is adopted for such recoupment of revenue from the States, the recommendations of the Finance Commission will be workable. This aspect will have to be examined by the NEDC.

35. Any problem in the working of the arrangements concerning flow of development finance from the financial institutions should be looked into by the sub-committee of Finance of the Standing Committee of the NEDC.

36. No change in the existing procedure of channeling external aid for projects is suggested. However, much misunderstanding would be avoided if at the time of consideration of the Five Year Plan, all relevant factors taken into consideration in this regard are placed before the NEDC.

37. The seasonal range of Weekly Ways and Means 'demand' compared to the prescribed limits should be carefully studies every year for the proceeding triennium in the light of price-trends, separately for each State, by the Reserve Bank and taken into account in re-fixing quarterly Ways and Means limits for the State. The period of over-draft should be extended from 7 to 14 days in view of the prevailing time lag in collecting relevant information from various Treasuries. Simultaneously, steps should be taken to modernize the treasury system.

38. The following two proposals may be considered by the Union Government:
    (a) Free foreign exchange to the extent of a small fraction of a State's annual budget should be placed at its disposal. This will introduce flexibility which will help reduce much of the present limitation.
    b) In each state capital and in the head quarters of remote but important districts of the bigger States, a designated officer of the State Bank of India (or some other nationalized bank) should be given power of Deputy Controller of Foreign Exchange of the Reserve Bank of India, in case an office of the Reserve Bank itself is not located there. This will go a long way to help the local public, especially small and medium businessmen.
39. It will be useful if the Union Government appoints and Expert Team to look into the special difficulties of the people in remote states an district in matters like the issue of shares, bonds, licenses, permits, etc. for which they have now to come to New Delhi, and suggest measures for delegating the power to some officer or agency under its control all the head-quarters of each State and remote but important districts of the bigger States.
40. Flow of direct assistance and refinance through co-operatives and other institutions to agriculture and private enterprises in other sectors does not generally fall within the ambit of Union-State financial relations. However, given the over-all development and equity considerations, it is too important to be ignored. Undesirable politicization of the co-operative system, thus leaving untapped substantial institutional finance which could be available for development has been noted by expert studies. In the context of consideration of an institutional finance to the private sector, two aspects become pertinent. One is that scarce capital resources in our country carry a high opportunity cost. Therefore, their optimum use is a must. The second aspect is that notwithstanding the preferential and concessional finance facility offered, people in the less-developed States have not been able to avail of the institutional finance to the desired extent. It is necessary to develop organizational capabilities and enterprise urgently in such States.

## CONCLUSION

The recommendations of the Sarkaria Commission with respect to financial relations between the Union and the States constitute the most important part of all the recommendations. The federal structure in our country, to begin with, was heavily weighted in favour of the Centre Over the years, the series of constitutional amendments and various legislative measures taken 'in the public interest' by the Central Government titled the balance further against the States. With more regional parties being voted to power in the States, the federal super structure of our country will be put to test more frequently, seen in the backdrop, the recommendations of the Sarkaria Commission assumes an important place so as to evolve a prudent policy mix in the area of federal financial relationships.

The Commission has taken favourable view on the demand of the States to have financial resources at their disposal. Inclusion of Corporation Tax in the divisible pool will go a long way to ease the resource problem of the States. At the same time, the suggestion to periodically review and explore the revision or imposition of duties covered by Article 268 will also make available more resources to the States.

The Expert Commission with representation from the States, as suggested by the Sarkaria Commission will go to a long way towards appropriately changing the tax structure and federal financial relations in consonance with changing circumstances. In fact, this Committee is only a part of the entire Institutional changes suggested by the Sarkaria Commission. A standing Finance Committee of the NEDC has also been recommended. Besides, in order to maintain close liaison between Finance Commission and the Planning Commission, it has been suggested that Finance Commission Cell/Division may be located in the Planning Commission. So this cell will continuously monitor the behavior of States' Finances. Thus, it will be possible to keep track of deviations from the forecast and suggest corrective measures.

Effective measures for decentralization have been suggested by the Commission on Centre-State Relations. The State Level Finance Commission to suggest district/region-wise allocation of financial resources within a State will help bring about balanced regional development.

In order to maintain the sanctity of Finance Commission, it has been suggested that the Union Government should not, as far as possible, deviate from there commendations of a Finance Commission. If such departure is essential, the compelling circumstances must be made clear easy flow of relief in the wake of natural calamities has also been suggested.

Taking on overall view, we can say that the Sarkaria Commission has recommended an appropriate federal-financial structure encompassing diverse factors like more resource devolution for the States, maintaining strict financial discipline on part of the Union and the States, creation of new Institutions to suit the changing circumstances. All these will provide a sound base for finance Commissions to commence these work, as well as any impending controversy between the Union and the States, will have to be solved in the light of the work carried out by the sarkaria Commission.

Sarkaria Commission Report is pending before the Government since 1987. Recently, in the month of September, 1992, the government has appointed a sub-committee to seek ways and means to implement the recommendations of the Sarkaria Commission. Rajasthan Chief Minister said on September 14, 1992 that undue delay in implementing the Sarkaria Commission recommendations has caused irrecoverable financial loss to the states. He estimated the loss of revenue to Rajasthan to the tune of Rs. 225 on royalty of minerals and Rs. 1,000 cores due to non-sharing of corporation tax. He expressed his concern over the slow progress of discussion on the recommendation of the Sarkaria Commission.

## Notes and References

1. R. Datt and K.P.M. Sundaram, Indian Economy, 1991, p. 729.
2. *Ibid*, p. 731.
3. *Ibid.*, p. 733.
4. Mishra and Puri, Indian Economy, p. 942.
5. *Ibid.*, p. 944.
6. *Ibid.*, p. 945.
7. Quoted in Faidia and Minaria, Sarkaria Commission Report and Centre-State Relations, Sahitya Bhawan, Agra, 1990, p. 33.
8. Madhu Limaye, Contemporary Indian Politics (New Delhi, 1987), p. 42.
9. Report of the Commission on Centre-State Relations, Part-1, p. 264.
10. *Ibid.*, p. 269.
11. *Ibid.*, p. 271.
12. *Ibid.*, p. 274.
13. *Ibid.*, p. 275.
14. *Ibid.*, pp. 276-277.
15. *Ibid.*, p. 281.
16. *Ibid.*, p. 281.
17. *Ibid.*, p. 284.
18. *Ibid.*, p. 285.
19. *Ibid.*, p. 285.
20. *Ibid.*, p. 286.

21. *Ibid.*, pp. 286-87.
22. *Ibid.*, p. 287.
23. *Ibid.*, p. 289.
24. *Ibid.*, p. 290.
25. *Ibid.*, p. 291.
26. *Ibid.*, p. 291.
27. *Ibid.*, p. 293.
28. *Ibid.*, p. 294.
29. *Ibid.*, p. 295.
30. *Ibid.*, p. 295.
31. *Ibid.*, p. 296.
32. *Ibid.*, p. 296.
33. *Ibid.*, p. 297.
34. *Ibid.*, p. 298.
35. *Ibid.*, p. 301.
36. *Ibid.*, p. 301.
37. *Ibid.*, pp. 301-02
38. *Ibid.*, p. 306.
39. *Ibid.*, p. 309.
40. *Ibid.*, p. 309.
41. *Ibid.*, p. 310.
42. *Ibid.*, p. 310.
43. *Ibid.*, p. 311.
44. *Ibid.*, p. 312.
45. *Ibid.*, pp. 313-14.
46. *Ibid.*, p. 314.
47. *Ibid.*, p. 314.
48. *Ibid.*, p. 314.
49. K.K. George and I.S. Gulati, "Central Inroads into State Subjects", *Economic and Political Weekly*, August 6, 1985, p. 601.
50. *Eeconomic Times*, August 28, 1992.

# *Summary, Conclusion and Recommendations*

## SUMMARY AND CONCLUSION

Federalism is a modern concept which is the result of historical evolution. It springs from the necessity for the Union of a number of independent states which are not strong enough individually to protect themselves from outside danger and whose Union is requisite for their safety and for promotion of their economic interests, but which are not prepared to surrender their independence completely. The impulses which lead to the formation of a federation are usually the idea of national unity the desire to promote common economic interests and the amicable resolution of common problems and considerations of defense and international prestige. The federal form of government is not reduced from a theory or a prior reasoning, but is a historical product or a necessity arising under certain political conditions. Its fundamental principles have been fully worked out in the most highly developed federation in the world, that of U.S.A.

The framers of the Indian constitution have mainly been influenced by the provisions of the American, Canadian and Australian federations. Some scholars describe India as a quasi-federal State, and some even regard it as more unitary than federal.

There are three models of federalism—Unitarian, cooperative and bargaining. There is a distinction of degree rather than kinds in these models. Sometimes all these models are visible in a political system in comparison to each other. Under Unitarian federalism, union governments developed their powers at the cost of regional governments. The main forces are five-fold-was and depression, welfare, technical, grants-in-aid party politics. Regional governments live in a perpetual condition of financial difficulties and stand like beggars at the door of centre. The Union and state governments in India arte virtually controlled by all powerful party in a way that our federal pattern has become a matter of form while its spirit has become unitary under the rule of Congress Party.

Under cooperative federalism, not only distribution of powers but also sincere cooperation between the union and state government clearly witnessed. "Planning in India is a co-operative enterprise in which the basic norms of development are set by centre in discussion with the states, a large amount of finance is provided by the centre and the main administration machinery is supplied by the states". Utilization of water resources and financial co-operation are also example of co-operative federalism. Many of the welfare functions of the states would suffer if large financial cooperation does not come from the centre.

Indian federalism has also evolved conference techniques facilitating small union state relations and inter-level cooperation. Periodical conferences between the representatives of the Union and state have become a regular feature of operation machinery of Indian federalism. The value of these meetings lies in adoption of an integrated and cooperative approach towards the solution of the numerous problems which arise under Indian federal structure.

Under bargaining federalism party system and federalism become closely related. In developed nations consensus among the political parties is seen but third world nations lack it. Due to multiplicity of parties, national party rules in centre and regional party rules the states. In India, bargaining federalism was found after fourth Lok Sabha Elections when non-congress and regional parties came into power in states. Presently this bargaining process has caught deeper roots, yet it will take time to have matured-decision on bargaining power of the states.

In federal system the functions and duties of the state are divided between the centre and state governments and they are generally defined in the constitution. Allocation of functions may create problems in the allocation of resources between centre and state corresponding to their requirements. Thus, the fundamental problem of federal finance is ensuring that the division of revenue between central and regional governments corresponds with the distribution of functions in order that each government may have the functional capacity to carry out its responsibilities as far as possible. On the consideration of administrative efficiency almost all important and elastic sources of revenue are allocated to federal government and on the ground of autonomy states are assigned expenditure on social and developmental items. Thus, federal government has the resources and the states have responsibilities. This creates the problems of fiscal adjustments which are as follows:

(a) The union governments has become most formidable fiscal and financial agency having substantial taxing power and large resources while states have emerged as helping hands of the centre in Task of National development.
(b) Transfer of resources from centre to states has been increasing. States are becoming more dependent on union.
(c) Centre has acquired the large number of control measures over states by transferring of funds.
(d) Disproportionate aid to poorer states is given by centre for a variety of social, political and economic reasons.

In the recent past, discontent of states has been increasing over the allocation of funds. As the non-congress states governments have grown, this discontent has also increased. M.V. Pylee advocated the following guiding principles for transfer of resources:

> "The basic principles that guide the allocation of resources between the federation and the unit's efficiency, adequacy and suitability".

B.P. Adarkar added three guiding principles for fiscal adjustment—independence and responsibility, Adequacy and elasticity and administrative economy and efficiency.

Anyway, the problem of fiscal adjustment should be solved by an approach of reality and pragmatism so that a healthy financial relation may develop.

Union-state financial relations in India may be studies in three phases; (i) before India Act, 1935, (ii) India Act, 1935, (iii) Constitution of India. This has been dealt with in detail in the previous chapter. Our constitution provides a clear cut division of taxing power. Both the union government and the states have been provided with independent sources of revenue. Parliament can levy taxes on the subject included in Union List I (23 items as mentioned in Seventh Schedule from item 82 to 92A and from 22 to 40). The state can levy taxes, on the subjects in the State List II (19 items from item 46 to 64 of Seventh Schedule). There is no Concurrent List. Besides these, the following three categories are mentioned in the constitution:

(a) Taxes levied and collected by the Union, but assigned to states. Article 269 mentions such six items.
(b) Duties levied by the Union but collected and appropriated by the States. Article 268 mentions such items.
(c) Taxes and duties which are to be levied and collected by the Union, but the proceeds shall be distributed to the States in a prescribed manner. Article 270 mentions such items.

One of the instruments which the constitution has evolved for the purpose of distributing financial resources between centre and states is the Finance Commission (Article 270, 273, 275 and 280). The Finance Commission, according to Article 280 of the Constitution, is constituted by the President once every five years and is a high-powered body. The duty of the Commission is to make recommendations to the President as to—

(a) The distribution between the Union and the States of the net proceeds of taxes which are to be or may be, divided between them and the allocation between the states of respective shares of such proceeds.
(b) The principle which should govern the grants-in-aid of the revenue of the States out of the Consolidated Fund of India.
(c) The continuance or modification of the term of any agreement entered into by the Government of India with the Government of any State specified on Part B of the first schedule under Clause (1) of Article 278 or under Article 306.
(d) Any other matter referred to the Commission by the President in the interest of sound finance.

The Tenth Finance Commission has been constituted under the chairmanship of K.C. Pant on 15th of June, 1992. The four other members are: (i) D.P. Pal (former High Court Judge and presently M.P.), (ii) BPR Vithal (expert of Finance and account of Government), (iii) C. Rangarajan (Economist), and (iv) M.C. Gupta (expert of finance and administration). Some controversy has arisen over the nomination of economist and High Court Judge. Both come from the official side and from independent. If all members represent centre and none is to look after the interest of the States. This is aggravated the anxiety of non-congress state governments.

Like Ninth Finance Commission, Tenth Finance Commission has invited severe criticism over the "term of reference". There is no mention of "normative" approach in the term of reference, but Dr. Raja J. Chellian and others in a seminar, "Issues before the Tenth Finance Commission" have suggested that 'normativeness' is implied in the Term of reference. A summary of appointment, Recommendations duration, and Head of the Finance Commission will explain the situation:

| *Finance Commission* | *Appointed* | *Submitted Report* | *Duration* | | *Chairman* |
|---|---|---|---|---|---|
| First | 1952 | | 52-53 | 56-57 | K.C. Neogy |
| Second | June, 1956 | 1957 (Final) | 57-58 | 61-62 | K. Santhanam |
| Third | Dec., 1960 | Dec., 1962 | 62-63 | 65-66 | A.K. Chanda |
| Fourth | May, 1964 | Aug., 1965 | 66-67 | 68-69 | P.V. Rajamannar |
| Fifth | March, 1968 | July, 1969 (Final) | 69-70 | 73-74 | Mahabir Tyagi |
| Sixth | June 28, 1972 | Nov., 1973 | 73-74 | 78-79 | K. Brahmanand Reddy |
| Seventh | June, 1977 | Oct. 28, 1978 | 79-80 | 83-84 | J.M. Shetal |
| Eighth | June 20, 1982 | April 30, 1984 | 84-85 | 88-89 | Y.B. Chavan |
| Ninth | June 17, 1987 | June 30, 1989 (Final) | 89-90 | 94-95 | N.K.P. Salve |
| Tenth | June 15, 1992 | Nov. 30, 1993 | 95-96 | 99-2000 | K.C. Pant |

Planning Commission, a non-statutory permanent body has surpassed the Finance Commission, a statutory but *ad-hoc* body as former recommends Two-third of the proceeds of central government and letter only one-third. This has viciated the situation and overlapping of recommendations makes a difficult position. In order to ensure coordination between Finance Commission and Planning Commission, for the first time, Dr. B.S. Minhas, member Planning Commission was appointed as a part time member of the Sixth Finance Commission. Finance Commission has limited itself only to the non-plan distribution of share of taxes and grants-in-aid, the Planning Commission is concerned with plan grants and the union government itself makes independently for both of them. Thus, devolution of fund on the

| *Plan and Period* | *Shared Taxes* | *Grants* | *Loans* | *Total* |
|---|---|---|---|---|
| 1950-51 | 53 | 32 | 73 | 158 |
| First Plan (1951-56) | 344 | 288 | 799 | 1431 |
| Second Plan (1956-61) | 668 | 789 | 1411 | 2868 |
| Third Plan (1961-66) | 1196 | 1304 | 3100 | 5600 |
| Annual Plan (1966-69) | 1282 | 1389 | 2676 | 5347 |
| Fourth Plan (1969-74) | 4562 | 3831 | 6708 | 15101 |
| Fifth Plan (1974-79) | 8337 | 8153 | 3801 | 25208 |
| Sixth Plan (1980-85) | 23730 | 15470 | 11250 | 50450 |
| Seventh Plan (1985-90) | 48000 | 41400 | 15000 | 104400 |

*Sources*: Seventh Finance Commission, pp. 172-73 and Ninth Finance Commission.

recommendations of Finance Commission is known a statutory, on the recommendation of Planning Commission is termed as developmental and by the centre Government as discretionary. The following table will provide a consolidated picture of resources transferred by the centre to the states:

The transferred resources from centre to states come nearly to 45 percent of the total expenditure of the states. The growing transference of resources reveals the following results:

(a) Centre-state finance have increasingly been integrated,
(b) States are helpless before the centre for fund, and
(c) Centre has been increasingly power over states.

Increasing amount of loans has aggravated the non-congress state governments. This is the case with grants also. Share of taxes; have also gone up during the ensuing plans. This shows that increasing yields of various taxes have tempted the central government to rule bluntly over the states. The states find themselves in hard financial position to implement the welfare programs for the masses. Not only this, they have their own resources very meager and so most of the non-congress state governments are crying to enhance the resources.

To find out the amicable solution of the tense centre-state relations, the Government of India appointed Sarkaria Commission in 1983 which submitted its report in January 1988. The summary of the report exhibits that the commission to preserve the unity of the country, rejected the suggestions to reduce the functions of centre or modify them. All the recommendations of the commission have been thrown into light but no actions have been taken in this regard. In September 1992 the Government had constituted a sub-committee to seek ways and means to implement the recommendations.

## RECOMMENDATIONS

For better and healthy centre-state financial relations we may recommend the following:

(1) There must be a clear-cut demarcation of the relative scope and function of the Planning Commission and Finance Commission.
(2) Planning Commission should be made a statutory body, making necessary amendment in the constitution.
(3) Centre-State Financial relations should be reviewed from time to time by a Permanent Body.

(4) Finance Commission should be given permanent status so that follow on thought may be undertaken to the problem of Centre-State Financial Relations. This will enable substantial gain in efficiency.

(5) The permanent Finance Commission will see the proper implementation of the accepted recommendations. The staff of this permanent body should be non-political to pay a watch and advisory role.

(6) There should be a statistical research cell on Public Finance on the lines of the work done by Australian Commonwealth Grants Commission to provide adequate statistical information.

(7) Corporation tax should be included in the divisible pool of income tax so that increasing demand of fund by the states may be met out.

(8) Principles for determination of grants-in-aid to the states be calculated on the basis of per capita income and the relative tax efforts of the state which is measured by tax per capita tax revenue as a proportion of per capita income.

(9) In determining the grants-in-aid, the difference between state per capita income and average per capita income, actual tax efforts and ideal tax efforts and budgetary gaps should also be taken into consideration.

(10) Basis of distribution of Union Excise Duty should be 90% population and 10% economic backwardness of the state.

(11) General criteria for distribution of taxes shows population and collection.

(12) The power to collect taxes levied under Article 269 of the Constitution be granted to states. It will substantially boost the Treasury of the state.

# Appendices

## Table 3A
## Resources Transferred by the Centre to the States

| *Plan* | *Plan Period* | *Shared Taxes* | *Grants* | *Loans* | **Total** |
|---|---|---|---|---|---|
| ------------ | 1951-52 | 53 | 32 | 73 | 158 |
| First Plan | 1951-56 | 344 | 288 | 799 | 1431 |
| Second Plan | 1956-61 | 668 | 789 | 1411 | 2868 |
| Third Plan | 1961-66 | 1196 | 1304 | 3100 | 5600 |
| Annual Plan | 1966-69 | 1282 | 1389 | 2676 | 5347 |
| Fourth Plan | 1969-74 | 4562 | 3831 | 6708 | 15101 |
| Fifth Plan | 1974-79 | 8337 | 8135 | 8810 | 25282 |
| Sixth Plan | 1980-85 | 23730 | 15470 | 11250 | 50450 |
| Seventh Plan | 1985-90 | 48000 | 41400 | 15000 | 104400 |

*Source*: Report of the Seventh Finance Commission.

## Table 3B
## Sharing of Income Tax Proceeds

| *Finance Commission* | *%age share in the divisible pool* | | *%age share of UTs/Part C States in (3)* | *%age share of states in (3)* | *Distribution of (5) amongst States: weights assigned to* | | |
|---|---|---|---|---|---|---|---|
| | *of Centre* | *of State & UTs/Part C States* | | | *Population* | *Collection* | *Assessment* |
| *(1)* | *(2)* | *(3)* | *(4)* | *(5)* | *(6)* | *(7)* | *(8)* |
| First | 45 | 55 | 2.75 | 97.25 | 80 | 20 | |
| Second | 40 | 60 | 1.00 | 99.00 | 90 | 10 | |
| Third | 33.33 | 66.66 | 2.50 | 97.50 | 80 | 20 | |
| Fourth | 25 | 75 | 2.50 | 97.50 | 80 | 20 | |
| Fifth | 25 | 75 | 2.60 | 97.40 | 90 | | 10 |
| Sixth | 20 | 80 | 1.79 | 100.00 | 90 | | 10 |
| Seventh to Ninth | 15 | 85 | 2.19 | 100.00 | 90 | 10 | |

*Source:* Reports from the Finance Commission.

## Table 3C
## Sharing of Excise Duty

| *Finance Commission* | *States' share of excise duty* | *Distribution of excise duty on the basis of* | |
|---|---|---|---|
| | | *Population* | *Other affecting factors* |
| First | 40% of 3 duties | 40 | 60 |
| Second | 25% of 8 duties | -- | -- |
| Third | 20% of 35 duties | -- | -- |
| Fourth | 20% of 45 duties | 80 | 20 |
| Fifth | --do-- | 80 | 20 |
| Sixth | --do-- | 75 | 25 |
| Seventh | 40% of all duties | 25% weight for four factors | 25% weight for four factors |
| Eighth and Ninth | 45% of all duties | | New Formula |

*Source:* Reports from the Finance Commission.

TABLE 3D
**Sharing of Union Excise Duty**

| *States* | *Percentage Share* |
|---|---|
| Andhra Pradesh | 8.208 |
| Arunachal Pradesh | 0.073 |
| Assam | 2.631 |
| Bihar | 12.418 |
| Goa | 0.110 |
| Gujarat | 4.550 |
| Haryana | 1.244 |
| Himachal Pradesh | 0.595 |
| Jammu and Kashmir | 0.695 |
| Karnataka | 4.928 |
| Kerala | 3.729 |
| Madhya Pradesh | 8.185 |
| Maharashtra | 8.191 |
| Manipur | 0.171 |
| Meghalaya | 0.208 |
| Mizoram | 0.073 |
| Nagaland | 0.096 |
| Orissa | 4.326 |
| Punjab | 1.706 |
| Rajasthan | 4.836 |
| Sikkim | 0.030 |
| Tamil Nadu | 7.931 |
| Tripura | 0.303 |
| Uttar Pradesh | 16.787 |
| West Bengal | 7.976 |
| **Total** | **100.000** |

*Source:* Reports from the Ninth Finance Commission.

TABLE 3E

## Addition Duties of Excise in Lieu of Sales Tax

| *States* | *Percentage Share* |
|---|---|
| Andhra Pradesh | 7.170 |
| Arunachal Pradesh | 0.897 |
| Assam | 3.810 |
| Bihar | 11.028 |
| Goa | 0.523 |
| Gujarat | 3.183 |
| Haryana | 1.099 |
| Himachal Pradesh | 1.943 |
| Jammu and Kashmir | 3.548 |
| Karnataka | 4.104 |
| Kerala | 3.087 |
| Madhya Pradesh | 7.224 |
| Maharashtra | 5.185 |
| Manipur | 1.171 |
| Meghalaya | 0.891 |
| Mizoram | 1.109 |
| Nagaland | 1.348 |
| Orissa | 5.358 |
| Punjab | 1.362 |
| Rajasthan | 5.524 |
| Sikkim | 0.269 |
| Tamil Nadu | 6.379 |
| Tripura | 1.556 |
| Uttar Pradesh | 15.638 |
| West Bengal | 6.600 |
| **Total** | **100.000** |

*Source:* Reports from the Ninth Finance Commission.

TABLE 3F

**Addition Duties of Excise in Lieu of Sales Tax**

| *States* | *Percentage Share* |
|---|---|
| Andhra Pradesh | 7.680 |
| Arunachal Pradesh | 0.107 |
| Assam | 2.743 |
| Bihar | 8.317 |
| Goa | 0.228 |
| Gujarat | 5.905 |
| Haryana | 2.317 |
| Himachal Pradesh | 0.621 |
| Jammu and Kashmir | 0.929 |
| Karnataka | 5.865 |
| Kerala | 3.723 |
| Madhya Pradesh | 7.164 |
| Maharashtra | 11.886 |
| Manipur | 0.213 |
| Meghalaya | 0.190 |
| Mizoram | 0.068 |
| Nagaland | 0.120 |
| Orissa | 3.486 |
| Punjab | 3.533 |
| Rajasthan | 4.689 |
| Sikkim | 0.052 |
| Tamil Nadu | 7.064 |
| Tripura | 0.278 |
| Uttar Pradesh | 14.657 |
| West Bengal | 8.165 |
| **Total** | **100.000** |

*Source:* Reports from the Ninth Finance Commission.

TABLE 3G

**Percentage Share of Each State in the Grant of Repeated Tax on Railway Passenger Fares**

| *States* | *Percentage Share* |
|---|---|
| Andhra Pradesh | 7.484 |
| Arunachal Pradesh | 0.008 |
| Assam | 1.509 |
| Bihar | 8.266 |
| Goa | 0.133 |
| Gujarat | 5.717 |
| Haryana | 1.637 |
| Himachal Pradesh | 0.098 |
| Jammu and Kashmir | 0.520 |
| Karnataka | 3.271 |
| Kerala | 3.562 |
| Madhya Pradesh | 6.061 |
| Maharashtra | 22.634 |
| Manipur | 0.013 |
| Meghalaya | 0.040 |
| Mizoram | -- |
| Nagaland | 0.165 |
| Orissa | 1.614 |
| Punjab | 3.110 |
| Rajasthan | 4.579 |
| Sikkim | 0.004 |
| Tamil Nadu | 6.893 |
| Tripura | 0.042 |
| Uttar Pradesh | 15.437 |
| West Bengal | 7.203 |
| **Total** | **100.000** |

*Source:* Reports from the Ninth Finance Commission.

TABLE 3H
**Grant-in-Aid**

| *States* | *Amount of Grant ( Rs. Crores)* |
|---|---|
| Andhra Pradesh | 64.50 |
| Arunachal Pradesh | 1.50 |
| Assam | 22.50 |
| Bihar | 26.25 |
| Goa | 0.75 |
| Gujarat | 63.75 |
| Haryana | 12.75 |
| Himachal Pradesh | 13.50 |
| Jammu and Kashmir | 9.00 |
| Karnataka | 20.25 |
| Kerala | 23.25 |
| Madhya Pradesh | 27.75 |
| Maharashtra | 33.00 |
| Manipur | 0.75 |
| Meghalaya | 1.50 |
| Mizoram | 0.75 |
| Nagaland | 0.75 |
| Orissa | 35.25 |
| Punjab | 21.00 |
| Rajasthan | 93.00 |
| Sikkim | 2.25 |
| Tamil Nadu | 29.25 |
| Tripura | 2.25 |
| Uttar Pradesh | 67.50 |
| West Bengal | 30.00 |
| **Total** | **603.00** |

*Source:* Reports from the Ninth Finance Commission.

## TABLE 31
## Grant-in-Aid—Article 275(1)

| *States* | *Total 1990-95 (Rs. Crores)* | *1990-91 (Rs. Crores)* | *1991-92 (Rs. Crores)* | *1992-93 (Rs. Crores)* | *1993-94 (Rs. Crores)* | *1994-95 (Rs. Crores)* |
|---|---|---|---|---|---|---|
| Andhra Pradesh | 341.25 | 46.07 | 54.60 | 66.54 | 78.49 | 95.55 |
| Arunachal Pradesh | 302.79 | 57.65 | 59.45 | 60.76 | 61.48 | 63.45 |
| Assam | 874.23 | 205.61 | 179.68 | 172.87 | 161.42 | 154.65 |
| Bihar | 1374.27 | 185.53 | 219.88 | 267.98 | 316.08 | 384.80 |
| Goa | 166.58 | 33.66 | 33.31 | 33.06 | 32.88 | 33.67 |
| Himachal Pradesh | 523.09 | 133.75 | 109.67 | 104.50 | 98.32 | 96.85 |
| Jammu and Kashmir | 1096.42 | 210.99 | 213.60 | 224.35 | 220.87 | 226.61 |
| Kerala | 412.54 | 55.69 | 66.01 | 80.45 | 94.88 | 115.51 |
| Madhya Pradesh | 1047.81 | 141.45 | 167.65 | 204.32 | 241.00 | 293.39 |
| Manipur | 371.65 | 74.92 | 74.90 | 74.40 | 73.32 | 74.11 |
| Meghalaya | 256.18 | 58.88 | 50.32 | 51.27 | 48.54 | 47.17 |
| Mizoram | 379.79 | 74.75 | 76.22 | 76.16 | 90.54 | 89.51 |
| Nagaland | 458.67 | 92.26 | 92.48 | 93.88 | 90.54 | 89.51 |
| Orissa | 1082.98 | 146.20 | 173.28 | 211.18 | 249.09 | 303.23 |
| Punjab | 53.91 | 7.28 | 8.63 | 10.51 | 12.40 | 15.09 |
| Rajasthan | 1446.79 | 195.32 | 231.49 | 282.12 | 332.76 | 405.10 |
| Sikkim | 84.68 | 17.59 | 17.37 | 17.03 | 16.50 | 16.19 |
| Tamil Nadu | 43.79 | 5.91 | 7.01 | 8.54 | 10.07 | 12.26 |
| Tripura | 466.01 | 101.19 | 101.27 | 96.52 | 87.25 | 79.78 |
| Uttar Pradesh | 3235.10 | 436.74 | 517.62 | 630.84 | 744.07 | 905.83 |
| West Bengal | 998.65 | 134.82 | 159.78 | 194.74 | 229.69 | 279.62 |
| **Total** | **15017.18** | **2396.26** | **2614.22** | **2962.02** | **3276.08** | **3768.60** |

*Source:* Reports from the Ninth Finance Commission.

# Bibliography

## Books


Adarkar, B.P., Principles and Problems of Federal Finance, P.S. Knig and Sons, London, 1933.

Agarwal, P.P., The System of Grants-in-aid in India, Asia Publishing House, Bombay, 1959.

Agarwal, R.N., Financial Committee of Parliament, S. Chand, New Delhi, 1966.

Agarwal, S.N., Indian Public Finance, Vora & Co., Allahabad, 1967.

Ambedkar, B.R., The Evolution of Provincial Finance in British India, 1925.

Bomwell, R., Federal Financial Relations in India, Minakshi Prakashan, Meerut, 1970.

Bhatnagar, S., Union State Financial Relations and Finance Commission, Chugh Publication, Allahabad, 1979.

Bhargawa, P.K., Essays on Indian Public Finance, Chugh Publication, Allahabad, 1978.

Bhargawa, P.K., Centre-State Financial Relations, Constitutional and Parliamentary Studies, 1973.

Bhatia, H.L., Centre-State Financial Relations in India, Birla Institute of Scientific Research, New Delhi, 1979.

Bhatia, H.L., Public Finance, Vikas Publication, New Delhi, 1980.

Basu, H.B., Federalism, Finance and Social Legislation in Canada, Australia and U.S.A.

Basu, D.D., Introduction to the Constitution of India, Prentice Hall of India, New Delhi, 1985.

Chanda, A., Federalism in India, George Allen and Unwin, London, 1965.

Government of India, Ministry of Law and Justice, Constitution of India, 1985.

Government of India, Ministry of Information and Broadcasting, India, 1991.

Gopal, M.H., Studies in Indian Public Finance, Asia Publishing House, Delhi, 1971.

Gyan Chand, The Essentials of Federal Finance.

Havajon, A.H., The Process of Planning: A Study of India's Five Year Plans, Oxford University Press, London, 1966

Institute of Constitutional and Parliamentary Studies: Federal Financial Publication in India, 1974.

Jagmohan (ed.), Twenty-five Years Indian Independence, Vikas Publishing House, New Delhi, 1973.

Khan, M.Y., Indian Financial System: Theory and Practices, Vikas Publishing House, New Delhi, 1980.

Menon, K.V.S., Task set for the Sixth Finance Commission, Free Press, Bombay, 1972.

Misra, B.R., Indian Federal Finance, Orient Longmans, Kolkata, 1963.

Panigrahi, D.D., Centre-State Financial Relations in India, Vikas Publishing House, New Delhi, 1985.

Rao, V.K.R.V., Centre-State Finance Relations, Institute of Social and Economic Changes, Bangalore, 1973.

Roy, Bharti, Evolution of Federalism in India, Progressive Publishers, Calcutta, 1976.

Santhanam, K., Transition in India, Asia Publishing House, Bombay, 1964.

Sah, K.T., Federal Finance in India, D.B. Tarperawala and Sons, Bombay, 1929.

Sinha, R.K., Fiscal Federalism in India, South Asian Publishers, New Delhi, 1980.

Sinha, R.K., Evolution of Federalism in India, South Asian Publishers, New Delhi, 1980.

Singh, Baljeet, Federal Finance and Underdeveloped Economy.

Shastri, K.V.S., Federal State Fiscal Relations in India, Oxford University Press, 1966.

Tripathi, R.N., Federal Finance in Developing Economy, Sterling Publishers, New Delhi, 1980.

Tripathi, A.N., Federal Finance and Economic Development in India, Sterling Publishers, 1985.

Thomas, P.J., The Growth of Federal Finance in India, Oxford University Press, Madras, 1939.

Varma, R.P., Federal Financial System in India, Standard Publication, Maz, 1979.

Vakil, C.N., Financial Development in Modern India, D.B. Tarperawala and Sons, Bombay, 1924.

Whear, K.C., Federal Government, Oxford University Press, London, 1946.

### Reports

Report of the Eighth Finance Commission.

Report of the Ninth Finance Commission.

Report of Sarkaria Commission.

Eighth Five Year Plan (1992-97).

### Articles

Thakur, A.K., Finance Commission, Yesterday, Today and Tomorrow, Civil Service Chronicals, September 1992.

Misra, S.K., Tenth Finance Commission: Beyond Mere Stabilization, E.T., July 25, 1992.

Ahmed, S.T., Finance Panals and the Union Government I & II, E.T., 24th and 28th August, 1992.

Thimmaiah, G., Finance Commission: Skewed to the Centre, E.T., August 3, 1992.

Thimmaiah, G., State's Fiscal Deficit Relevance, E.T., August 15, 1992.

### Editorial

*Economic Times* (New Delhi), June 17, 1992, An Appropriate Agenda for Tenth Finance Commission.

*Hindustan Times*, The Tenth Exercise, June 17, 1992.

# Index

Any Satisfactory Extent, 146
Audit and Accounts, 39

Bargaining Process under Federal Set-up, 20
Borrowing and Audit, 39
Borrowing Powers, 46
Brief Survey of Union-State Fiscal Relation before of India Act, 1935, 32
Centre-State Conflicts on Finances:, 136
Channel of Transfer, 71

Channels of Union-State Transfers in India, 71
Characteristics of Federal Systems, 11
Commission and Finance Commission, 133
Commission in India, 120
Comparison of Ninth and Tenth Finance Commission, 129
Concept of Fiscal Federalism, 1
Customs and Excise Duties, 64

Demarcation of the Functions of Planning
Developing Nations, 50
Distribution of Estate Duty, 99
Distribution of Grants-in-aid in India, 111
Distribution of Tax on Railway Passenger Fares, 102

Economic Interpretation of Federalism, 19
Emergency Provisions, 67

Failure to Tackle the Problem of Regional Imbalance to
Federal Finance and Economic Development, 27
Federal Finance in Australia, 57
Federal Finance in Canada, 53
Federal Finance in Underdeveloped Countries, 60
Federal Grants to States, 65
Federal Inter-Regional Transference of Resources and Development, 25
Federal Principles, 9
Finance Commission and Planning Commission, 124
Financial Agreements in Developing Countries, 63
Financial Power of the Governor, 40
Financial Power under Indian Constitution, 46
Financial Provisions under Government of India Act, 1935, 36
Fiscal Federalism in USA, Canada, Australia and Developing Nations, 50

Grant on Account of Wealth Tax on Agricultural Property, 105
Grants-in-Aid in Australia, 59
Grants-in-Aid in Canada, 54
Grants-in-Aid in India, 106
Grants-in-Aid in Lieu of Jute Export Duty, 98
Grants-in-Aid in U.S.A, 51
Guiding Principles of Fiscal Adjustments, 24

History of Feseralism and the Federal Idea, 3

Income Tax, 41, 64
Inter-Governmental Financial Institutions, 67

Jewish Communities of Europe, 5

Krishnamachari, T.T., 125

Latin American Federalism, 14

Modern Approaches, 6

Nature of the Indian Federal System, 17
Need of Transfer of Resources, 71

Modern Approaches, 12

Political Base of Fiscal Federalism, 1
Problem of Fiscal Adjustments, 23
Problems of Less Developed State in India:, 144

Recent Trends, 70
Reduced Importance of Finance Commission, 146
Regional Imbalances as a Source of Conflict, 141
Resource Transfers, 47
Responsibility and Resources of the Centre and of the States, 137
Review of Financial Relations, 43

Sarkaria Commission: , 147
Separation in Australia, 57
Separation in Canada, 53
Separation in U.S.A., 50
Sharing of Additional Duties of Excise, 91
Sharing of Income Tax in India, 73
Sharing of Union Excise Duties, 81
Sources of Conflict Listed by the States, 138
States Complaint on Financial Arrangements, 139
Statutory Sources:, 72

Tax-Sharing in Australia, 58
Tax-Sharing in Canada, 54
Tax-Sharing in U.S.A., 51
The Centre's Case, 142
The Duration of Finance Commission and the Presidents, 124
The Government Borrowing, 66
The Problem of Co-ordination Between Finance Commission and Planning Commission in India, 129
The Question of State Autonomy, 145
The Role of Grants-in-Aid, 108
The States' Demand, 141
Transfer for Resources through Finance

Union-State Conflicts, 136
Union-State Fiscal Relation in India, 32

View Point of the States, 147
Viewpoint of the Union, 151